ALSO BY LEVI LUSKO

Through the Eyes of a Lion: Facing Impossible Pain, Finding Incredible Power

Swipe Right: The Life-and-Death Power of Sex and Romance

I Declare War: 4 Keys to Winning the Battle with Yourself

tAKE BACK YOUR LIFE

A 40-DAY INTERACTIVE JOURNEY TO THINKING RIGHT SO YOU CAN LIVE RIGHT

LEVI LUSKO

W PUBLISHING GROUP

AN IMPRINT OF THOMAS NELSON

Published in Nashville, Tennessee, by W Publishing, an imprint of Thomas Nelson.

Published in association with the literary agency of Wolgemuth & Associates, Inc.

Thomas Nelson titles may be purchased in bulk for educational, business, fundraising, or sales promotional use. For information, please email SpecialMarkets@ThomasNelson.com.

Any internet addresses, phone numbers, or company or product information printed in this book are offered as a resource and are not intended in any way to be or to imply an endorsement by Thomas Nelson, nor does Thomas Nelson vouch for the existence, content, or services of these sites, phone numbers, companies, or products beyond the life of this book.

ISBN 978-0-7852-3276-6 (HC)
ISBN 978-0-7852-3277-3 (eBook)
ISBN 978-0-7852-3570-5 (ITPE)

Library of Congress Cataloging-in-Publication Data

Library of Congress Control Number: 2020937456

Printed in the United States of America

20 21 22 23 24 LSC 10 9 8 7 6 5 4 3 2 1

Thank you, Jesus, for a
seat at your table and for
giving me the power to win
the war against the version
of me I don't want to be.

CONTENTS

WEEK 3: CROSS THE BARBED WIRE

WEEK 4: RUN TOWARD THE ROAR

WEEK 5: BE THE DIFFERENCE

WEEK 6: THINK RIGHT, LIVE RIGHT

BEFORE

It is difficult to get your head around the immensity of the Panama Canal. I devoured a six-hundred-page book David McCullough wrote about it while on a family vacation last summer. Let me share some of my favorite takeaways. Each lock, if stood on end, would be taller than the Eiffel Tower. The amount of dirt that had to be removed was enough to make a Great Wall of China–style barrier that would stretch from New York City to San Francisco. If you laid all the dirt on an area the size of a city block, it would reach nineteen miles into the air. The canal uses twenty-six million gallons of water to lift a ship the six hundred feet required to pass through the locks.

The importance of this water causeway, which connects the Pacific Ocean to the Atlantic so ships can pass through without having to sail around South America, cannot be overstated. It takes eight to ten hours to sail through the canal, compared to the two weeks it took to go the long way. Using the canal saves eight thousand miles on voyages between one coast of North America and ports on the other side of South America. It has been called "one of the supreme human achievements of all time."

The construction of the canal involved many different nations, including the French who originally undertook it, the Americans who finished it, the Panamanians who revolted from Colombia and declared themselves emancipated and thus an independent country, and, of course, Colombia, who lost the privilege of owning it. At one point, twenty-four thousand people from ninety-seven countries were simultaneously working on it. In all, the fifty-mile stretch took thirty years to complete.

Then there is the way the Panama Canal connects with major world events. The lock chambers were built to accommodate the *Titanic*, then the biggest ship in the world. But she sank in 1912 and never got the chance to navigate the canal. The first time a sitting United States president ever left the country while in office was when Teddy Roosevelt took a trip to Panama to check on the canal's progress. Amazingly, only three Secret Service agents were sent to protect him. Despite the endless amounts of fascination that had been given to the project throughout its many decades of work, almost no attention was given to its inauguration, because just as the first ship crossed from one ocean to the other through the canal—August 3, 1914—World War I erupted.

The US and France spent almost $639 million to build the canal, making it the most expensive thing built in American history to that point. In lives, it was much more expensive: a staggering twenty-five thousand people died to create the passageway, ten times the number of people who died in the September 11 attacks. You heard me right. That's five hundred lives for every mile of the canal's fifty miles. The primary causes of those deaths were malaria and yellow fever, which were especially rampant in the hospitals. Nearly everyone who was sent to a hospital died of one of these diseases. It was so well known that being hospitalized was a death sentence that at some points people begged to not be taken to the hospital, regardless of how badly injured or sick they were.

We know today these diseases are blood-borne infections, but that wasn't common knowledge in the late nineteenth and early twentieth centuries. In those days, people thought the illnesses were caused by gasses contained in the ground that were released by digging. It was widely believed that since the diseases originated in the dirt, ants were a primary cause of infection. So ants became public enemy number one. The canal management launched a massive campaign to keep the ants away from people, especially those who were sick or who showed signs of weakened immune systems.

Since ants can't swim, one preventative measure involved placing all four legs of hospital beds into shallow pans of water, creating liquid barriers that kept the ants from climbing up to the patients. Little moats were dug around existing fruit trees as well. The standing water was incredibly effective at keeping ants away—but people kept dying anyway.

The problem, of course, is that ants do not carry yellow fever or malaria. On the other hand, mosquitoes do. And do you know what mosquitoes love? Water, especially stagnant standing water like that found in these Panamanian gardens and hospital rooms. So many mosquitoes lived in t   tals that a set of doctors or nurses had to fan their working colleague   the insects at bay. Mosquitoes were laying their larva and thriving. Th   ats—the very things people thought were keeping them safe—were co   m their lives.

I can relate. Too many times to count, I've made the   e of doing the right thing the wrong way. Traded the eternal for the t   y. Fought the ants but fostered the mosquitoes. By telling myself tha   one addiction is keeping me connected, I have allowed it to isolate me. By following my feelings, I have become trapped in moods that should have not had a hold on me. By failing to take my thoughts captive, I have allowed anxiety to have a seat at the table reserved only for God and paid for with the blood of his Son. What I have looked to for joy has pried it from my fingers. I have learned the hard way—and I am still trying to remember—that it's not only possible but also easier than ever to gain the whole world (wide web) and lose your true self.

I have a feeling you can probably relate. Do you ever feel like you are losing control? Losing your peace? Losing your mind? Have you screamed at your kids and then felt terrible? Said something horrible to your spouse that had nothing to do with how you felt about your loved one but everything to do with how you felt about you? Have you turned to spending or drinking to take the edge off a low moment, only to feel worse when the morning found you hungover in your mind and waiting on your credit card bill? That is what happens when we turn to idols that have eyes but cannot see, ears but cannot listen, and arms but cannot save.

Perhaps when you think of idols, you think of a demonic gold statue. But idolatry is very, very sneaky. Idols can be sheets with a high thread count, bucks with a high point count, or a game with a high score count. Idols aren't usually bad things; they are good things that are treated as *ultimate* things. Your idol might be your clean home, your social media standing, your career, or what your friends think about you.

What you look to for hope might just be immersing the legs of your bed in pans of water. There's not an ant around for miles, but the mosquitoes are having a field day. But there is good news: you can take back your life.

When people finally figured out the connection between stagnant water, mosquitoes, and disease, they removed the water and added screens to their windows. The mosquitoes went away, and with them so did the malaria and yellow fever. The drop was so precipitous it was staggering. During the twenty years the project was under French control, a staggering twenty-two thousand people died. Once the mosquitoes were nailed as the culprit, only three thousand additional people died in the final ten years, and many of these were killed in accidents.

Fighting the battles of life is not enough; you must fight the right way. I want to help you figure out how to do that. That is what this journey is all about.

Jesus instructed his disciples to gather up the excess fish and loaves after he fed the five thousand, and as a result, the disciples had twelve full baskets to take with them on to the Sea of Galilee. In the same way, I've combed through my notes from when I was writing two previous books—*Through the Eyes of a Lion* and *I Declare War*—and gathered up the best of the leftovers for this project. Some are my favorite moments from the books; others are sections that were edited out. Rereading the material God gave me allowed me to identify some mosquito bait I have allowed to creep back into my story; in addition, it helped me with issues that weren't a struggle for me in a previous season. I also came across some ideas I wished had made it into the books, so I included them in this project.

Instead of being collected in twelve baskets, this journey is broken up into forty days. Life supposedly begins at forty. It sure did for Moses, who spent the first forty years of his life thinking he was somebody, the second forty years of his life finding out he was nobody, and the final forty years of his life discovering what God can do with somebody who knows he is a nobody. All across Scripture, the number forty comes up again and again. In Noah's day, rain fell for forty days and forty nights (Genesis 7:4). The spies sent by Moses to explore the promised land did so for forty days (Numbers 13:25). The Israelites after the generation of the exodus wandered in the wilderness for forty years (Numbers 32:13). Goliath taunted the Israelites for forty days before David cut him down (1 Samuel 17:16). Jesus fasted forty days and forty nights in the desert (Matthew 4:2). Forty days was the period from the resurrection to the ascension (Acts 1:3). And through these forty days I believe God is going to do something significant deep inside your soul that will mark you forever.

A few days ago, my wife pointed out to me that our door hinges were squeaky. Our two-and-a-half-year-old baby boy, Lennox Alexander Lusko (named after his big sister Lenya Avery Lusko, whom he has yet to meet) kept waking up early in the morning when he might have otherwise slept longer, because of the afore-mentioned squeaky hinges. Out to the garage I went, and I came back with a can of WD-40 in my hand. Problem solved.

As I lubricated the hinges, I thought about how this magic little can earned its name. As the story goes, a chemist, Norm Larsen, was trying to come up with a formula to prevent corrosion—a job done by displacing water. He failed thirty-nine times but then finally figured it out on the fortieth try. The house-hold brand WD-40 stands for "Water Displacement perfected on the 40th try," a testimony to the power of perseverance.

As you embark on this quest to displace the mosquitoes from your life, don't be discouraged if you don't see progress right away, or even if it feels like you take four steps forward and then five steps back. The growth you're after won't be easy or come quickly, but it will come if you don't give up. I believe you will see progress in your life if you stay the course.

Rather than simply read this book, I want you to answer the questions and take the time to allow God to speak to you. I have included Breathe, Think, and Live sections at the end of each day so that you can do exactly that. Don't blaze through it in a rush. This experience isn't about checking a box; it's about changing your life. Going through the material with a small group would be a powerful experience; the accompanying curriculum and video sessions (available separately) will take this journey to an even deeper level.

But at the end of the day, it won't work if you don't work it. The Mandalorian can do all he can, but Baby Yoda still has to do his part to stay alive. If you give yourself to this process, I really believe things could look a lot different forty days from now.

Leave the ants alone. It's time to swat some mosquitoes.

WEEK 1

LOOK IN THE MIRROR

Day 1

1

HIDING IN PLAIN SIGHT

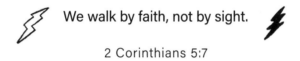 We walk by faith, not by sight.

2 Corinthians 5:7

In 2011, the FBI ended the most extensive manhunt in the bureau's history when James "Whitey" Bulger was caught. The mob boss from Boston had been on the run for sixteen years, but they finally nailed him. Sixteen years is a long time. Get this: he spent a majority of his time on the run at the number-two spot of the FBI's top ten most wanted list. Number one was Osama bin Laden.

He was second only to Osama. That's how badly the Federal Bureau of Investigation wanted to find this man. And when he was finally found, he wasn't in some cave in some far-off country. He was in Santa Monica, California, living three blocks from the beach in an apartment. Hiding, *60 Minutes* reported, in plain sight.

60 Minutes interviewed the apartment manager. They interviewed the next-door neighbors. And these people had *no idea*. They thought Bulger and his girlfriend were a nice retired couple living on a tight pension. They didn't seem remarkable in any way. But the neighbors had no idea this guy had $800,000 socked away inside the walls of the apartment. They had no idea he had an arsenal of semiautomatic and automatic weapons and hand grenades. They had no idea Johnny Depp was going to be cast to play him when the movie of this man's life was made. They had no idea he was wanted in connection with more than nineteen murders. That he, at one point in his life, had killed someone with his own hands and had then taken a nap. He was that jacked up.

When the neighbors were asked, "What sticks out to you about him?" they said he was nice to cats.

There's your first tip-off that something's wrong.

But let me say this: these people saw one thing. What was really there was another thing altogether. A very serious thing. I want you to notice that this is constantly happening in our lives too. Looks can be deceiving.

We can look at something but not see what's there. And that means we cannot trust what we see with the naked eye. This is how Paul put it in 2 Corinthians: "So we fix our eyes not on what is seen, but on what is unseen, since what is seen is temporary, but what is unseen is eternal" (4:18 NIV).

We fix our eyes—fix our gaze. I'd say our gaze is broken, but when we focus on the right things it's fixed. We're also choosing to fix it. As in "fixing a stare"— that is, focusing our energy and concentration. For the things we see now will soon be gone, but the things we cannot see will last forever.

What's Paul saying in this verse? He's saying you can't trust your physical vision. You can't trust what you see and the decisions you make based on that. *You need more.*

FOR THE THINGS WE SEE NOW WILL SOON BE GONE, BUT THE THINGS WE CANNOT SEE WILL LAST FOREVER.

Truth be told, we walk around oblivious to much of what's going on. We click our pictures, double-click on Instagram. Scroll, scroll, double-click. Scroll, scroll, double-click. Scroll, scroll, double-click. But as we have our sips of latte and watch our movies and read another issue of whatever magazine, we have no idea much of the time who and what is watching us and what is actually happening. There is a whole spiritual realm with very serious things going on. There is a whole eternity ahead of us. There is life after death. There is an actual all-out war going on all around us, a war for our hearts, lives, and souls. But we can't see it because we've got a blind spot. And that blind spot is taking our lives from us.

In this journey, we'll start to open our eyes to what's going on beyond the obvious. We'll start seeing what's really there. And we'll be empowered to change for the better ourselves and the world we live in. We'll search out and know the truth, and the truth will set us free.

Second Corinthians 5:7 says, "We walk by faith, not by sight." If you walk around trusting what your eyes are seeing, your blind spot will continually lie to you. Then you pick up the night-vision telescope called faith. And instead of just trusting what you see, you look through its lens, and it changes everything. You can see in the dark. You can see what's coming against you. And you can see what's right in front of you, what's working *for* you.

When you look at people, what are you going to see? You're going to see potential. You're going to see they're destined for impact. They were made in the image of God. There is amazing potential packed inside of them—and inside you too. You're going to look at people and realize there's no such thing as an ordinary person. You've never met a normal person in your life. Everybody you see is part of a royal priesthood, a chosen generation (1 Peter 2:9). So, to borrow so[...]ds from Loki, brother of Thor, you're going to look by faith at people an[...]meone who is *burdened with glorious purpose.*

[...]hen you see problems, you'll automatically assume that God's working[...]s together for your good. When you look at them with the naked eye, no[...]ch. But when you look through the lens of faith, you're not going to get di[...]ged, because you're going to remember that God has a plan.

How about when you experience pain? You're going to look at it and believe that God is going to give you great power because it is a grace to suffer. And along with suffering comes the grace to go through it and to get something out of it. God's going to do great things through the pain, and you're going to know you're not alone in the midst of it.

When you go through what you're going through, the same God who walked with Adam in the cool of the day is going to walk with you through it. Then you can say, *I know that you're with me. I am not alone, and I will fear no evil, even here in the valley of the shadow of death.* Through faith, eternity becomes visible. When you operate in faith, you know that what you see is not the end of the story.

You may not be happy with your story right now. You may be disappointed or grieving or bored, or maybe you've forgotten you're living a story at all. But you are. And together we will uncover what has been hidden in plain sight. With faith as your lens, I guarantee you that what you are going to see is going to blow your mind. It's going to show you that you can reach out and take back your life from whatever is sucking it away behind the scenes. And it's going to show you a whole new way of looking at the world.

When you can see the invisible, you can do the impossible.

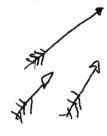

Prayer

Father, teach me to see what is hidden in plain sight. Fill me with faith and clear my vision so I can see my life through your eyes. Please bless me today so I can bless others. Amen.

 BREATHE, THINK, AND LIVE

- Has anything given you the sense there is more going on around you than meets the eye? Is that hard or easy for you to believe?
- How would you describe the story of your life right now? Is it a story you like? How do you feel about it?
- Where would you like your story to go?
- How would you describe your faith right now? Does anything keep you from accepting that God has plans for you that will involve a shift in your vision?
- What do you need to take back your life from? What's clouding your vision and making you focus on the here and now?

Day 2

‖

IDENTITY CRISIS

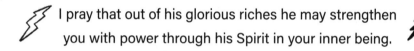 I pray that out of his glorious riches he may strengthen you with power through his Spirit in your inner being.

Ephesians 3:16 NIV

Before we can do the great things we're called to do out there, we must get things squared away on the inside. I'm talking about the war within. The Bible says that as a man thinks in his heart, so he is (Proverbs 23:7). There's great power to what takes place in our hearts and minds.

The sports world has long since recognized this power of harnessing the mind. In fact, in study after study, it has been proven that athletes who are of a similar physical disposition and given the same physical tools to train with will always excel and surpass others if they're also given a psychological component to their training. If they're trained to be not only physically tough but also tough in their minds. They need a mental edge.

This is true not only in athletics. In the business world, executives receive training to deal with the high-stakes decisions they have to make in the organizations they lead. Soldiers and law-enforcement officers are given tools to deal with critical stress management and how to still perform well when the stakes are high.

Like it or not, we all have a battle that we're constantly fighting. We talked about opening our eyes to the war we're in. There are many battles in that larger war happening outside and within us. I want to start, though, with a look in the mirror. I want to start with the battle that is taking place on the inside.

It's what James was talking about when he said, "What is causing the quarrels and fights among you? Don't they come from the evil desires *at war within you?*" (4:1 NLT). He's saying, *Something's going on, something more than just what you're facing from outside influences.*

Things don't go the way we want them to go. We don't do what we meant to do. When the stakes are high, there's turmoil, there's pressure, and we blow it. Even if we've been practicing on a friendly home court, the game has completely changed. We're not in Kansas anymore.

Paul said much the same thing. In Romans 7:15 we read, "I don't really understand myself" (NLT). I love that sentence. Can't you picture Paul looking in the mirror, being like, *Who are you? I don't even know you and I* am *you.*

I'm with Paul. Sometimes I look at myself and ask, *Who even are you?*

He goes on, "For I want to do what is right, but I don't do it." Have you ever asked yourself, *Why did I do that?* Me too. "Instead, I do what I hate. . . . I love God's law with all my heart. But there is another power within me that is at war with my mind" (vv. 15, 22–23).

It's not just me, Paul, and James. We're all dealing with the civil war inside our souls. We're conflicted. We feel not completely sure what's the right thing to do or even to want. We feel like there's a traitor in our midst and it's us. *I've seen the enemy and it's me.*

We talked about how athletes and soldiers have to get the mental edge to deal with all they have to deal with. The funny thing is, in the New Testament, the two analogies that are most commonly used to describe what it means to follow Jesus are—you guessed it—being a soldier engaged in warfare and being an athlete who's running to win the prize. So it is for us as it is for both soldiers and athletes; the calling is great and the pressure is high.

I mean, we've been given the most important assignment that's ever been given to anyone: *take this message of the gospel of Jesus and get it to every part of the world.* And it's the only hope of saving mankind. Talk about stress! The clock is ticking. Time is running out. Life is racing by. Only what's done for Christ will last. That's pressure.

Yes, there are outside components to this. The devil and the world. The Bible says we have enemies. We'll definitely talk about that. But we have enough problems to deal with, including the fact that we tend to self-sabotage. And we are more than capable of becoming our own worst enemies.

So I believe we have a great need for what Paul prayed for the church at Ephesus, that they would be strengthened in the inner being, according to the riches of his glory (Ephesians 3:16). That's my prayer. That at the very outset of this journey, God, through his Holy Spirit, will strengthen us in our inner beings. That he will walk with us as we get wise to these battles and take back ground from the Enemy.

If this feels like the start of an identity crisis for you, good! Because the best kind of crisis you can have is an identity crisis, where you begin the process of learning who you truly are. Fighting. Asking questions. Before you can fully do what you're called to do, you must finally understand who you're called to be. And that's the awakening, the revelation that every believer needs to have.

A huge component in mental training in athletics is crafting the proper self-image. If you imagine yourself to be a failure because you lost your last game or you didn't live up to your own expectations, you will eventually prove yourself right. In fact, one expert who has trained many major league players said, "You can't outperform or underperform your self-image for long. The self-image will eventually regulate behaviors and outcome."

Now let's take this into the Christian paradigm. How a man thinks of himself, so he is, says the Bible (Proverbs 23:7). Your thinking of yourself proves to be a self-fulfilling prophecy.

The Bible says we experience an identity shift the moment we become Christians. We are "in Christ." In Christ, we are tucked. In Christ, we are enveloped. It's as though we're placed under an umbrella of grace, and now what previously would hit us can't hit us because we're covered by Christ.

When we were struggling to win, striving to achieve, straining to please God, Jesus said, essentially, "The message of the gospel isn't try; it's trust. You don't have to carry the weight of what you can do for me; just stand on the strength of what I have done for you."

Once you're under that umbrella called grace, how God views you, your identity, doesn't change day to day with your behavior or with your activity. You don't have to get a good-behavior gold star on the big star chart in the sky or revile yourself when you mess up. Now, just as an athlete would say to themselves, *I'm fast, I'm strong, I'm unstoppable, I've got the eye of the tiger,* you can know who Jesus says you are.

What if you woke up every day, looked at yourself in the mirror, and proclaimed what God says about you? You are loved. You are chosen. You are called. You are equipped.

But I had a bad week . . .

Loved. Called. Chosen. Equipped.

But I haven't been a good husband . . .

Loved. Called. Chosen. Equipped.

Every day. It doesn't change, because God doesn't love you more on your best day or less on your worst day. That's why I want to push you into an identity crisis. It's the only place you can truly experience the relentless love of God.

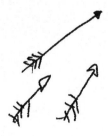

Prayer

Father, rid me of the selfish parts of my old identity that pull me toward sin. Remind me and strengthen me in who you say I am. Amen.

BREATHE, THINK, AND LIVE

- ✗ Think of times when you felt the war within yourself. When you caved under pressure. When you did something you did not want to do, like Paul. (I know it's depressing, but I promise it'll get better.)
- ✗ In what situations do you most often tend to blow it?
- ✗ How does it feel to chew on the idea that God loves you *exactly as much* in those times as he does when you're doing awesome?
- ✗ What do you tend to do to put good-behavior stars on your star chart in heaven?
- ✗ How does it feel to know that God loves you *exactly as much* then as he does when you are blowing it in the worst way?
- ✗ What are some direct consequences being "in Christ" can have on your self-image? Will it make you more _____? Or less _____? (Fill in the blanks.)
- ✗ What are you most looking forward to about developing that mental edge when you're battling with yourself? What do you hope will change?

Day 3

|||

YOU MATTER MORE
THAN YOU KNOW

 God created mankind in his own image, in the image of
God he created them; male and female he created them.

—Genesis 1:27 NIV

I don't know what you see when you look in the mirror, but if you are like me, there is a long list of things you wish you could change. When I first wake up most mornings, I splash water on my face, look at myself, and think, *Dude, you look like you got hit by a truck.* But lately there have been a lot of times when I have seen a sadness in my face that hasn't always been there.

Regardless of what you see looking back at you while you brush your teeth, I can tell you with zero hesitation that, to God, there is nothing ordinary about you. You might spit your toothpaste out just like everybody else, but the truth is, you are complex, special, and one of a kind. I realize I'm getting all Barney the purple dinosaur on you, but I'm dead serious. There is nothing even remotely close to normal about you.

It doesn't help that so much of our lives feels pretty unimportant, composed of activity that is seemingly insignificant. Folding clothes, writing papers, paying bills, watching *Seinfeld* reruns, eating dinner. Repeat. But don't let the simplicity of life fool you. You are so close to the details that it can be difficult to get perspective, but you are a part of a much larger story. You matter more than you know.

You might feel pretty ordinary or average. Maybe you've been picked on or squashed down by people. That gets old pretty quickly and eventually can cause you to believe what is being said about you. Even worse, maybe you have been flat-out told you are worthless. You feel tempted to accept that you are doomed to alcoholism (like your father before you) or divorce (like just about everyone you know). Hear me loud and clear: these are all lies!

Here's some truth for you brought to you by your new lenses, your new way of looking at yourself:

YOU WERE MADE IN THE IMAGE OF GOD. That's right, *made*. You are not smart mud or a monkey wearing pants. God made you. Fearfully, wonderfully, he knit you together inside your mother. You're no accident. Out of all creation, God made humans, male and female, to be like him. And as his image bearer, you possess a gift no animal was given: self-awareness. You have free will. You are not a robot or a puppet.

⬥ Need proof? See Psalm 139:13–14; Genesis 1:27; 5:2.

YOU HAVE AUTONOMY. Like God, you have a personality. A sense of humor. You can laugh and sing, make love and create, dream and destroy. You have feelings and can be hurt. When things don't go your way, you get sad and can be grieved, just like God. This might surprise you, but God doesn't always get what he wants and neither do we. Jesus knocks at the doors of our hearts, and we have to invite him inside in order to be saved. He is a gentleman, so he knocks. He won't go all SEAL Team Six and kick the door down. He gives us the dignity and responsibility of making our own decisions.

   ♦ Ephesians 4:30; Revelation 3:20; Galatians 3:14

YOU ARE IMMORTAL. The question is not whether you will live forever but where. Four hundred years from now, and four thousand years after that, you will still exist. You will still be alive, and you will still be you.

   ♦ John 8:51; 1 Corinthians 15; Luke 20:36

YOU WERE EXPENSIVE. Think about what God was willing to spend to redeem you and give you hope when sin and death had their suffocating stranglehold on your life. The value of something comes from what someone is willing to pay for it. And, boy, were you expensive! The Bible says that while we were dead in our sins, God demonstrated his love for us by sending his Son to die for us (Romans 5:8). You weren't purchased with any common currency, like gold or silver, but with the precious blood of Jesus. His veins were opened, and then, hanging on two pieces of wood on top of a hill shaped like a skull, the Son of

God died to pay the price for every wrong thing you have done. Sin is a capital crime, so he died to set you free.

There is no higher price that has ever been paid for anything in history. No Rolex, luxury yacht, penthouse apartment, work of art, or private island can come close to being as outrageously expensive as your freedom. You are valuable not just by birth but because blood was spilled so you could be born again.

    ✦ Romans 5:8; John 3:16; Luke 12:6–7; Ephesians 5:2

YOU HAVE POWER. As a child of God you have been entrusted with the Holy Spirit. The same Holy Spirit that raised Jesus from the dead now lives in your heart and is ready and waiting to be activated. Greater energy courses through you than can be measured with horsepower. As often as you ask, the Spirit is prepared to surge afresh into your soul, like the power coming from Iron Man's glowing chest piece, turbocharging your efforts as you rise up to do all God wants you to do.

    ✦ 1 Corinthians 3:16; 2 Timothy 1:14; Romans 8:11; Ephesians 3:16–20

YOU ARE GIFTED. Then there are the gifts and unique privileges you have been given. There are spiritual capabilities and also skills, talents, and abilities. He has made you passionate about certain things. You have specific connections and opportunities that I haven't been given. Remember, you're a genius. There are people you get to talk to every day whom it would take a miracle for a preacher to get in front of. But for you it's as effortless as sitting in second period or clocking in for an afternoon shift at your job. Lucky!

★ Ephesians 2:10; James 1:17; 1 Peter 4:10–11; Matthew 5:14–16

YOU HAVE AN EPIC MISSION. Oh, and did I mention, you have also been tasked with the greatest mission that has ever been undertaken in the history of the world: the Great Commission, a mission to go fishing. The orders from your commanding officer are pretty clear: go into all the world and preach the gospel to every creature. People who believe will be saved, but if they do not, they will not. You're pretty much like Frodo, except instead of a ring that has to get to the volcano, you have a message that is the only hope of saving mankind from sin and death. Basically, the most important thing ever.

★ Matthew 4:19–20, 28:16–20; Romans 10:14–15; John 15:16

So let's recap. The God who created the universe made you and trusted you with his image. The most important person ever to live was willing to die to save you. You are tapped into a power source greater than the electricity generated at Niagara Falls added to the mushroom cloud of Hiroshima, plus you have spiritual superpowers. Rule zero of the internet is "Don't mess with cats," and the number one rule of Fight Club is "Don't talk about Fight Club," but the most important thing to know about living up to your potential is that if you don't understand your calling, you will undervalue it.

I hope you are starting to get a sense of how incredibly, wildly unordinary you are. You, my friend, were put on this earth to make waves, disrupt the status quo, and kick over some stinking applecarts. You have everything you need to move forward and live an extraordinary life.

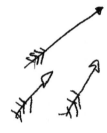

Prayer

Thank you, Jesus, for your death and resurrection, which has tapped me into an extraordinary, powerful, and purpose-driven life. Use me for your glory today. I am available. Amen.

BREATHE, THINK, AND LIVE

x When you read that you're special or one of a kind, what's your gut reaction? Hope? Excitement? Relief? Disbelief? Embarrassment? Did you roll your eyes? Get honest about the degree to which you believe you are actually, legitimately a big deal and that you matter. Reflect on why you react the way you do.

x When in your life have you felt you weren't made in the image of God? Think of a specific time someone told you that you were broken, funny looking, a screwup, fundamentally flawed. How does the fact that *you were made in the image of God* change any lies you may be holding onto from that time?

x When have you felt helpless, like you didn't have free will or a choice? How does the fact that *you have autonomy* change that?

x When have you felt you were temporary or that the things you do now just won't matter in the future? How does the fact that *you are immortal* change that?

x When have you felt you weren't worth much, that you were expendable, cheap, or disposable? How does knowing that *you were expensive* change that?

x When have you felt weak or powerless? How does knowing *you have power* change that?

x When have you felt average, dull, or untalented? How does the fact that *you are gifted* change that?

x When have you felt aimless, stuck, or ineffectual? How does that fact that *you have an epic mission* change that?

x Accepting the fact that you are wildly unordinary is the first step to taking back your life. From today, which *truth* hits you the hardest? Take the scriptures from that truth, maybe find even more, and dig in. Absorb them. Hang on to them for dear life as we move forward.

Day 4

||||

TORTURED GENIUS

 We are his workmanship, created in Christ Jesus for good works, which God prepared beforehand, that we should walk in them.

Ephesians 2:10 ESV

I want to give you some good news and some bad news. I'll start with the good. You—yes, you—are a genius.

Now I don't know how that sits with you. Maybe you're like, *I've always suspected it. Had my hunches. Thanks for that.*

Or maybe you're not quite so comfortable with thinking of yourself that way. I know if you were to tell me, "Hey, you're a genius," I'd be like, "Yeah, right. You should see my SAT scores. You wouldn't say that if you did."

But I think we have wrongly boiled down the meaning of genius, confining it to where it only refers to our IQ. We think of a genius as someone who is super-duper intelligent. Right? Albert Einstein, Thomas Edison—clearly geniuses. But let's think about our definition of that term. We need a bigger view of what the word can mean.

Check out the dictionary definition of the word *genius*: "A person who is exceptionally intelligent." Usually we stop and leave it right there. But the definition goes on: "A person who is exceptionally intelligent or creative, either generally or in some particular respect." Do you see how much more it opens up and has room to breathe?

Notice, too, how it says you can be a genius in *general* ways, meaning you're really smart or creative in a wide number of subjects. But then it gets more nuanced. We can be geniuses in a "particular respect." Meaning you can be a specialized genius, a genius when it comes to your particular turf. It doesn't just refer to the best and brightest in the country, a state, or even a city. You can be a genius on your cul-de-sac.

You only need to figure out where your genius lies. Where it is versus where it isn't.

Einstein is the go-to genius character. But check out what I read in a book by Seth Godin: "No one is a genius all the time. Albert Einstein had trouble finding his house when he walked home from work every day." Is that man a genius? *E equals mc squared . . . Now where do I live? I don't know.*

I read that he would often forget to wear socks. He clearly had no style. The hair was crazy madness. Is someone like Bear Grylls, who is a genius at navigation and can find his way by the stars but doesn't know anything about math, any less of a genius?

No, my friend. You are, in fact, a genius. And you have no choice or say in the matter.

That's who you are. That's how you were built.

We can see this from the very beginning of the Bible. Before God made human beings, he said this: "Let Us make man in Our image, according to Our likeness" (Genesis 1:26). That's how he made us: in his image and his likeness.

Right there's a huge clue. If we can figure out who God is, we can figure out a lot about who we are. We reflect him. Which raises the question: Who is God?

The fifth word of the Bible tells us. Genesis 1:1: "In the beginning, God *created*" (ESV). God is a creator. He starts with nothing. And when he's done with it, there's something. He starts with darkness. And when he has had his way, there is now light. There's only chaos and confusion. But when he's done with it, there's order and beauty and poetry and symmetry. And in his image, he made us both male and female.

Now we know something about ourselves. We were created to create by a Creator. Dreamed so that we might dream. Written in order to write. Sung into existence that we might sing. Crafted to craft. Engineered to engineer. Structured to structure. We were put on this earth by a creative God in order to be creative and to dream things into existence. Where there is nothing, there might be something. Where there is disorder, there might be order. Where there's only confusion, there might be rest and beauty.

Ephesians 2:10 says you are his workmanship. The word *workmanship* is the word *poeima* in Greek. It is where we get our English word for *poem*, but it also can be better translated as—get this—*masterpiece*. You're "his workmanship, created in Christ Jesus for good works, which God prepared beforehand, that we should walk in them" (ESV).

You are what happens when God gets to work on a project. And you are fearfully and wonderfully made. You get cut, you heal yourself. Your body's just like, "I got this. Plasma, platelets, healed." You're like an X-Man. He built you awesome. And he says, *Okay, now I've tucked your own personal genius within you, I've prepared works, and I want you to walk in them. I want you to figure out the nuanced way I've put my creative spark into your heart. And I want you to go on a cosmic scavenger hunt to figure out what fills your heart with passion that the world needs to have.* Then you begin to execute all these beautiful, one-of-a-kind acts of genius one at a time, and that puts a smile on the face of God.

Now that I've given you the good news that you're a genus, I have some bad news: you're a genius.

It's bad news because works of genius often come through great pain. You have to go through agony to birth something into the world that wasn't there before. It will cost you to create. There is conflict in every calling and angst inherent to the creative process.

The struggle is real because, in us, we have two natures: the fallen one and the one redeemed by God. And they're battling. We struggle to create works of genius because conformity is comfortable and taking risks is risky and greatness is not easy. It's always going to be harder to do the right thing than it is to do the wrong thing.

That's why checking your email a thousand times will always be easier than actually working on something. That's why scanning your Instagram feed is always going to be easier than actually doing something meaningful. That's why starting a project, with the blank screen staring back at you, is so hard.

But here's the thing. The harder you work, the better you get at getting over that hump and starting, and the harder it is to surrender.

Once you get fired up enough to make some progress—whether it's in getting out of debt, getting healthier, working on that business plan, writing that book, designing that bridge, or making that spreadsheet—the harder it is to quit, because you see what you've accomplished so far. You decide you're going to keep on or go down swinging.

We need that same kind of commitment to Jesus. In Matthew 10:38, Jesus said, "He who does not take his cross and follow after Me is not worthy of Me." He's saying, *You've got to love me with your whole heart. You've got to put me above everything else.* And that's the kind of conviction and commitment it's going to take not only to walk with Christ but also to see all of this genius come out of you.

Success isn't the immediate goal. Obedience always is. You will start winning these battles and taking ground when you know who you are and that you're doing what God calls you to do.

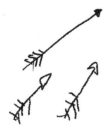 ## Prayer

Father, give me the strength to fight forward in my calling and to step into the beautiful things you've laid out before me. My goal is not perfection but progress. Amen.

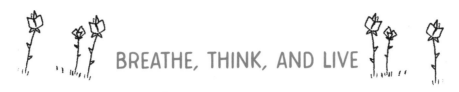

BREATHE, THINK, AND LIVE

- x How do you react to the news that you're a genius? Why do you think that is?
- x What might you be a genius at? What comes naturally to you? Even if you're not creative in an artsy sort of way, how do you display the qualities of bringing something out of nothing, order out of chaos? (This doesn't necessarily have to be in your job or career.)
- x What kind of resistance have you faced in creating? What struggles do you deal with in the bad-news part of being a genius?
- x When you think about taking back your life from the things that drain it away, how does the idea of getting over the hump help you? What humps do you need to get over to find the determination to see things through?
- x How might this "go down swinging" attitude apply to your faith as well as life? How can you remind yourself of it as you go through this journey?

Day 5

HHt

IF YOU SAY SO

Now the LORD God had formed out of the ground all the wild animals and all the birds in the sky. He brought them to the man to see what he would name them; and whatever the man called each living creature, that was its name.

Genesis 2:19 NIV

The first job God gave humans was to speak a word over something he made. Read today's verse. Did you catch what it said? Whatever man called the animal, "that was its name." Adam's job was to speak, and what he spoke stuck. You have the same job. God brings a day to you, and your job is to give it a name, to declare something over it. Whatever you call it will stick.

Think again about what you see when you look in the mirror. What do you choose to say in response to the person reflected there?

I am beautiful or *I am ugly*?

I am valuable or *I am not worthy of love?*

I am going to have a tremendous day or *I am so behind already?*

Whatever you say over what you see, that is what it is called.

Maybe, like me, you have gotten so good at listening to yourself that you have forgotten to speak to yourself. It's easy to drift along with the speakers of your soul blasting the play-by-play commentary of your naturally negative self.

If you're going to take back your life, you're going to need to fight for it.

It's time you fire yourself as your personal critic and rehire yourself as a coach. You can alter how you feel through changing the way you speak.

I woke up this morning to a worship song Alexa played for me on my Amazon Echo. I ate oatmeal and drank black coffee while I read my Bible and prayed. I haven't been on Instagram yet or purchased anything on Amazon. (If I reward my brain with dopamine before accomplishing anything, I'll be chasing that high all day; email and social media are a treat I allow myself only when I have done something worthy of the reward.) Now I'm listening to very carefully selected music, and I'm burning a candle I use only when I'm writing. I'm wearing a pair of nonprescription "writing" glasses, and when I put them on I am a writer who is not a coward or a procrastinator.

When I first woke up and thought about my writing, the usual intimidation began to tug at the edge of my mind: *You can't write. You'll get distracted. You tried to write on Monday but didn't get a single word out. No one—*

I muted that voice by speaking up: *This book is being written for the purpose of helping people change their lives. Writing it is going to benefit me and my readers. I can't wait to get started after I have my devotions. God has spoken to me, and he is going to speak through me!*

I forced these words to come out of my mouth (quietly, because it was 6:13 a.m. and my kids were asleep), but I needed to hear myself speak positivity over the day in front of me. Honestly, I don't have even a spare five minutes to sit around in fear, anxiety, and self-pity. Ain't nobody got time for that.

And with that I showed up and got to work. And you can too.

The specific things I did might not work for you. Perhaps you hate oatmeal, and candles give you a headache. That's okay. Figure out what fits you. You don't need to wear my author glasses to become the version of yourself you long to be. Maybe there is a special ring you put on that helps you become a kind mom. A special mug you drink your matcha out of that only brave, vulnerable, and self-aware people are allowed to touch. Taking back your life isn't one size fits all; it's a custom job for a tailor-made, one-of-a-kind masterpiece, because that's who you are and what your life is. You need to figure out what it takes for you to suit up so you can be your best when you show up.

Why do I say these things out loud? How you speak determines how you feel. It's time to stop listening to your fear! Instead, put some faith in the air. In the same way Disney imagineers designed the atmosphere of the Cars Land exhibit to make guests feel like they are on Route 66 in Radiator Springs, you should use your words to surround yourself with belief and strength.

I can't overemphasize the importance Scripture places on words. At the creation, God spoke the world into being (Genesis 1). At the incarnation, God spoke himself into the world, and the Word became flesh in the person of Jesus, the living Word (John 1:14). That should tell you something about the weight of words. At both the very beginning and then at the most critical, decisive moment in history, God's solution was to *speak*.

It should humble you to know God has given you the same power of speech. That is part of the terrible privilege of being made in his image. Your speech can create, tear down, build, heal, or hurt. When God hears you speak about your meeting as terrible, your car as crappy, your kids as ungrateful, your husband as lazy, your town as small, or your house as cramped, his response is, *If you say so.* Because of the power he put into your tongue when he made you, he will allow the labels you speak into existence to stick. Consequently, you will have a terrible experience in your meeting and an unenjoyable ride in your crappy car; you will find in your husband and kids a thousand examples of laziness and ingratitude; your house will indeed shrink around you, as will the suddenly claustrophobic town you are trapped in. You will feel how you speak and find what you seek.

On the other hand, you can choose to talk about the meeting as one that will be challenging but important, full of opportunities to solve problems. You can choose to talk about how you are grateful to have a car, how you are happy your husband works hard to provide for your family, and how your children are going to learn gratitude from your example. That reminds you that you are thankful you don't live in that tiny studio apartment anymore, and while your town may not be a booming metropolis, it's charming in its own way. That prompts you to pray for a neighbor who's been on your mind, and when you're done, you text her a few words of encouragement. God's response to this new way of speaking is the same: *If you say so.*

Your words can unlock a life you love or one you loathe. It is up to you whether the self-fulfilling prophecies you articulate become a delight or a dungeon. Fortunately, as C. S. Lewis wrote, "The doors of hell are locked on the

YOUR
WORDS CAN
UNLOCK A
LIFE YOU
LOVE OR
ONE YOU
LOATHE.

inside." If you talked your way into your current mess, you can very likely talk your way out of it.

As you start taking back your life, one of the first jobs you have is to speak life over yourself, as Adam did. Alter how you feel by changing what you say, and when you look in the mirror you'll begin to see you as you were meant to be.

Prayer

Father, thank you for the power you've placed in my tongue. Help me to steward it well. Fill my speech with faith so I can experience what Jesus died for me to have. Amen.

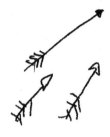 BREATHE, THINK, AND LIVE

- x Have you gotten so good at listening to yourself that you've forgotten to speak to yourself? If so, in what situations have you noticed this?
- x When have you noticed yourself using words to hurt, tear down, or complain about yourself in your day-to-day life? What would it mean to use them to build and heal in those areas?
- x If you were your own personal coach, pumping yourself up to become the person you want to be, how would that change your world? Walk

yourself through a typical day, hour by hour, and think about what this coach would whip into shape:

- at home
- at work
- in your relationships
- in your head

x Assuming oatmeal, candles, and author glasses aren't your thing (or even if they are), what small physical reminders can you choose to prompt you to speak positively and powerfully? To remind you that you are that person you need to be?

x Identify three negative things you find yourself saying in the mirror on a regular basis. These are things that keep you from showing up and getting to work.

Now write out your own positive responses.

The next time you find these negative thoughts running through your head, *speak your comeback out loud.* Force it out if you have to. Have no mercy on your internal critic.

Day 6

~~||||~~ |

MASK OFF

 For our boast is this, the testimony of our conscience, that we behaved in the world with simplicity and godly sincerity, not by earthly wisdom but by the grace of God.

2 Corinthians 1:12 ESV

You're out in public and you catch a glimpse of yourself. Maybe when you see your reflection gliding by a shop window or in the rearview mirror, or when you check your teeth for spinach after lunch. Today, squint a little harder. Is the *you* you're showing people really you? Or does your image feel a little disguised? A little distorted? A little masklike?

God tells us who we really are, but it can be hard to absorb, especially when fears hit. When pain or uncertainty push in, we forget. So we slap on a mask as a defense to hide the fears that we aren't enough—pretty enough, rich enough, strong enough, smart enough. The fears that we don't have what it takes, we aren't one of the cool kids, the lies and harsh words people have spoken over our lives are true. The fears that we're out of our league, inadequate, unqualified. We hide our pain. We hide our suffering.

Do you struggle with any of these things? Me too.

Which masks do you go for? You might need a whole closet of them, as each is suited for a particular situation. Here are a few of the most versatile.

- THE SUPERIORITY MASK. This could look like lashing out or criticizing, trying to make other people feel smaller because you feel small and misery loves company. But you can never rise up by cutting other people down. It doesn't achieve what you intend.
- THE SMILEY-FACE MASK. This one projects everything is cool, even though you're crying underneath. Often comes with the "I'm fine" defense, pretending sticks and stones don't hurt and acting as though you don't care what anyone thinks. But it is only a veneer covering up all the sadness within.
- THE "FIFTY SHADES OF GREY" MASK. Ramping up your sex appeal is another coping strategy. Going for ultrasexy outfits or pumping up your guns to get a *Baywatch* body by summer. You're seeking validation of your attractiveness, hoping for the approval that comes from being noticed.
- THE FUNNY GUY/GAL MASK. This is my big one. I need people to laugh, to think I'm amusing. I'm the class clown. If you turn everything into a joke or make self-deprecating remarks, this could be you. Humor serves as a deflection to divert attention away from what you feel insecure about.
- THE "I'M SO HOLY" MASK. People who hide behind their religion brag

about what they've done for God—for example, their service, their giving, how many Bible verses they know. Jesus responded to this directly: "You can't keep your true self hidden forever; before long you'll be exposed. You can't hide behind a religious mask forever; sooner or later the mask will slip and your true face will be known" (Luke 12:2 THE MESSAGE). We mistakenly believe God's blessings are determined by our behavior, but the truth is that his blessings come first, completely undeserved, and that is what helps us change our behavior. It's called grace. And it changes everything.

- THE CLONE WARS MASK. Trying to be like everyone else. It's like being in middle school, only it becomes more expensive as we get older. For instance, how much of our credit card debt comes from trying to stay on track with those in our peer groups and keeping up with the Joneses?

- THE ZOMBIE MASK. Numbing ourselves. Consuming drugs and alcohol, viewing pornography, overloading on social media, or compulsively shopping are like putting a zombie mask over our emotions. Why feel sad when you can have an instant hit of dopamine from Amazon Prime? The problem with numbing is that, to quote Brené Brown, "We cannot selectively numb emotions. When we numb the painful emotions, we also numb the positive emotions."

- THE GOLD-PLATED, DIAMOND-ENCRUSTED MASK. Compensation is the classic response to insecurity. It is famously demonstrated by Napoleon, who made up for his height with exaggerated bravado. Compensation looks like constant name-dropping, one-upping, bragging about your accomplishments, and turning everything into a competition. It's not only draining to those around you, but it's exhausting to keep up false pretenses.

It's ironic that we put on masks in hopes of finding love and acceptance, but people can't love someone they don't know. What they're falling in love with isn't you; it's your mask, a superficial version of you, a costume you've carefully curated.

What you wear to obtain, you must wear to retain.

If you get the job with the mask, you have to wear the mask every day at work. If you get the relationship with the mask, you have to wear the mask whenever you're with that person. "Fake it till you make it" is sometimes good advice, but when it comes to being fake as a way of covering over your insecurities, you never actually make it. If you fake it, you'll have to keep faking it.

Here's the real kicker. When you put on a mask, you are masking yourself from God's blessing.

You know masking tape? How when you paint a room, you first have to tape off the light switch, the ceiling, the floorboards? The paint only goes where the tape is not. That's why it's hard for God's blessing to reach what you've covered over. God constantly seeks to shower you with grace. He wants to cover you with favor, to coach you with his love, to give you his best and his blessings. He wants your cup to run over. He wants to anoint your head with oil. He has been dreaming about it from before the foundation of the earth. But he can't use who you wish you were, only who you really are. Your mask is holding you back.

Don't miss this! You are unique. You are beautiful, a work of art. You are God's poem. His masterpiece. You are what he thinks, not what you think.

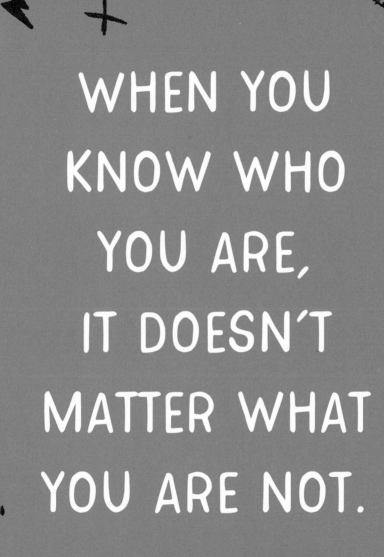

WHEN YOU
KNOW WHO
YOU ARE,
IT DOESN'T
MATTER WHAT
YOU ARE NOT.

The cure for insecurity is understanding your true identity.

When you know who you are, it doesn't matter what you are not. You are loved by God. That's why he made you, why he saved you. Why he shed the blood of his Son and filled you with his Spirit. Why he gave you a calling. You're loved by God! You don't need approval from anyone else, because the only likes that really matter come from heaven—and they are already yours.

The good news for us insecure, mask-wearing phonies is that we can choose to take our masks off. That's scary, I know. You might have been wearing one for so long you don't know what life would look like without it. But let me tell you: it looks like freedom.

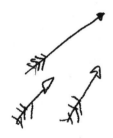

Prayer

Father, thank you for the freedom and fulfillment that comes from living life in the open. Give me the strength to live an unmasked life that is overflowing with your favor and blessing. Amen.

BREATHE, THINK, AND LIVE

- x What's your favorite mask? Do you have situational masks? What are they?
- x Have you ever gotten into a job, relationship, or social situation where

you started out inauthentic and then had to work to keep it up? How did that go?

x What do you think that mask is hiding? (You might have to think way back here to your childhood days.) A certain kind of insecurity? Pain? Shame?

x Thinking about what the mask is hiding, can you see any ways God might want to bring healing to that area? How does keeping the mask on keep that healing from happening?

x What would you look like if you dropped the mask? How would you interact differently with people? With yourself? With God?

x Your mask may be impressive, but it's nothing compared to the fearfully and wonderfully made authentic *you* that God made in his image and as his masterpiece. Pray that God will show you what that masterpiece really looks like the next time you're tempted to cover it up.

Day 7

HHt ||

PERMISSION SLIP

⚡ God gave us a spirit not of fear but of
power and love and self-control. ⚡

2 Timothy 1:7 ESV

Want to know what freedom looks like? What victory looks like? What comes after you've dropped your mask, when you get real with what's going on inside your head and start living in your true identity? You might be envisioning a "William Wallace on his horse" kind of freedom or a "Kate Winslet hanging over the rail of the *Titanic*" kind of freedom. And, hey, I wouldn't rule that out! But deep down, at its core, freedom looks like something unexpected. Something a little less glam.

Freedom looks like vulnerability.

The truth is that it takes bravery to be vulnerable. It's not easy, and you'll feel fear. You'll want to put the mask back on. You'll want to hide once more.

But in every area of life, the only way to get to victory is by going through vulnerability.

We are a glossed-over, fake generation. We either don't like who we are or we don't know who we are, so we make up an image of ourselves that we can pump out into the world in order to get likes and backslaps. We misrepresent what we see when we look at ourselves. Or we don't see anything worth opening up about. As a result, we've forfeited the vulnerability that is the only true means to the victory we desperately want.

Here's an example of how this works in marriage. My wife, Jennie, and I have talked a lot about being "naked and unashamed" within a marriage, getting back to what Adam and Eve were in the garden before all the "hiding behind fig leaves" stuff. You can unclutch your pearls; this is not just about wardrobe or lack thereof. It's about being known. It's about letting down the walls, telling your fears, telling your desires, telling your dreams, telling how you feel when you don't measure up.

It might look like a wife saying, "I'm looking for affection from you. I need to look for it from God. I only feel as good as you noticing me." It could be a husband saying, "I'm afraid I can't provide for our family. I'm afraid I don't have what it takes. I'm afraid I'm not worthy of your love." Whatever it is, we just gotta be naked and unashamed.

We also need vulnerability in the workplace. I believe it makes a team work better. People can say, "What you said hurt my feelings. I'm not going to lash out in anger and write an angry email to make you feel small because you made me feel small. I'm gonna tell you it hurt me. I'm going to try to get on with it."

You've got to have vulnerability in any act of creation—in art, music, or whatever it is where you're making something out of nothing or bringing order out of chaos. I had to find vulnerability when I learned to preach after God called me to speak and lead a church. There was a coming out of my khakis, I guess you could say; a shedding of some of the chrysalis of my upbringing to figure out what God wanted our church to be. I had to become comfortable and confident in that calling. I can guarantee you: whatever your calling is, you're going to have to be vulnerable to walk in it well.

It takes vulnerability to be ourselves and to be who God made us to be, to not be afraid to be naked and unashamed and exposed. And the truth is, if you live that way, people can claw at you. If you live with your heart out like that, there are going to be people who are going to hurt you. But we can't let that calcify our hearts or hold us back.

Instead, stay fresh, stay humble, and risk it again. Put yourself out there. Don't do work that is safe. Don't write songs you think everyone wants to hear. You gotta do you. It takes risk to be vulnerable. It takes bravery, but that's the only way to victory.

What happens if we pass on vulnerability? If we say no thanks? When we choose against vulnerability, what are we really choosing?

I'm going to give it to you straight: We choose cowardice. We choose fear.

I know this about you, without even knowing you: Fear is not a good look for you. It doesn't fit you. It wasn't given to you.

Paul was talking about this when he wrote to Timothy. Timothy felt afraid as he pastored the church at Ephesus. In the midst of success, he felt an insecurity, a turmoil within, a lack of confidence. We don't know all that it looked like. All we know is that he was struggling with cowardice. Feeling uncomfortable in his own skin. Believing that he didn't measure up or stack up or have enough. Timothy felt like we feel having to put on our Sunday best within, having to be someone we're not, having to live behind a mask and walls that we build up.

In essence, Paul reminded Timothy, "God didn't give you that spirit of fear."

The word "spirit" is the Greek word *pneuma* (*penuma*), like pneumonia, which is literally translated "breath" or "wind." Breathe out.

God didn't breathe fear into you, Timothy.

Think about it. What did God breathe into us? In the garden of Eden, he assembled dust and breathed his breath into our lungs. That's how we got life. At salvation, the Holy Spirit came like a wind. He breathed into our hearts, regenerating us with brand-new life. "You hath he quickened, who were dead in trespasses and sins" (Ephesians 2:1 KJV). Translation: you were dead, but now you're alive because of Christ—a brand-new creation!

When we look to God in the morning, when we look to God when we're struggling—*whoosh.* He breathes his Holy Spirit on us once again. God doesn't breathe into us fear or a lack of courage or a lack of confidence. He breathes into us life. He breathes into us resurrection power. He breathes into us what we need to do, what we've been called to do, as we've been called to do it.

Paul was basically saying to Timothy, "Don't go hide. Don't try to muscle through this in your own power. Don't put on any of your masks. No, that's not going to work. It's not going to be by might. It's not going to be power. *It's by my Spirit*, says the Lord."

You've got to let God breathe into your lungs. You got to let him breathe into your life. You've got to breathe out these insecurities. Open up in vulnerability.

Give back to God. "Cast all your anxieties on him," the apostle Peter wrote, "for he cares about you" (1 Peter 5:7 RSV).

If God didn't give it, you don't have to keep it. This is your permission slip to let that go. In this realm of insecurity, if you feel inferior and inadequate in your mind and heart, you can trust that God didn't give you that spirit of fear. So you can let it drop.

If God didn't give it to you, you don't have to keep it.

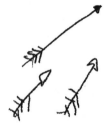

Prayer

Father, rid me of my insecurity, inadequacy, and inferiority mentality. Help me stay fresh, stay humble, and take risks over and over again. Amen.

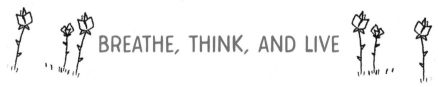

BREATHE, THINK, AND LIVE

× How have you seen vulnerability work in life? In relationships? In work?

× Have you ever been burned by vulnerability? What would it look like to get up and try again? What would that require of you?

× Would you consider yourself a courageous or brave person? Why or why not? How could vulnerability be an act of bravery as you step into your identity and calling?

x We have *all* made the choice for fear or cowardice at some point in our lives. Have you ever started to identify with fearfulness or cowardice? If so, in what way?

x How does it affect you to know that you are not identified with fear? That it's a wrong fit for you, not part of you, and you don't have to keep it?

x What did God breathe into you instead? How can you keep going back for more of that breath?

WEEK 2

tURN OFF tHE DARK

Day 8

tHt III

JESUS TURNS OFF THE DARK

 Jesus . . . has abolished death and brought life and immortality to light through the gospel.

2 Timothy 1:10

It was December 20, 2012, and I was writing my Christmas message. My wife and daughters were at a birthday party, so I buckled down to work out the details. Christmas Eve was only four days away. And working on this particular message felt like a struggle.

I'd gotten the idea for it a few weeks before, when Jennie and I were in New York to see the Spider-Man musical with friends. The experience was all right. A bit too much spandex and singing for my liking. But as we were walking out of the theater, lightning struck when I looked over my shoulder at the marquee and saw the big, bold letters: *Spider-Man: Turn Off the Dark.*

The words tumbled around in my mind, over and over. *Turn Off the Dark.*

Turn Off the Dark. Turn Off the Dark. It's an unusual phrase. You would usually say, "Turn on the light." You generally don't think about darkness being deactivated. But there we were, in Times Square, with all the chaos and flashing lights everywhere, and it hit me. "Eureka!" I announced to no one in particular. "There's my Christmas message! Turn off the dark." Back at the hotel I jotted down some notes and put the idea on ice.

Thursday, December 20, I pulled out those notes and spent the day locking in the message. My plan was to show that the light of Jesus' birth turned off the darkness of four things: loneliness, fear, despair, and guilt. These are darknesses we all struggle with daily. Jesus flipping the light on in these areas spoke to the hope of Christmas and to what Jesus, the wonderful counselor, had come to free us from.

I didn't realize it at the time, but the sermon was incomplete. It was missing a crucial point. Yes, Jesus turned off the darkness of loneliness, guilt, despair, and fear, but there was another thing he extinguished. By the end of the evening the final bullet point rudely pierced our home: death.

Death. Our great enemy. The last enemy. That day it didn't schedule an appointment or knock before entering. Death crashed our party. It punched us in the gut and left us breathless.

That night, December 20, 2012, our second-born daughter, Lenya Avery Lusko—our Lenya Lion—had an asthma attack. It was just a normal night, until all of a sudden it wasn't, and we ended up living our own worst nightmare. Lenya, after a painful time of not being able to breathe, eventually stopped breathing. And then, in my arms, her heart stopped beating. We couldn't bring her back. The ER doctors couldn't bring her back. On that cold Thursday night in December, at five years of age, Lenya Lion went from our lives to the arms of her heavenly Father.

Today, we are so thankful for the peace it brings to know that she's with Jesus. We're thankful for the hope that we had in the midst of those dark days. And yet I won't hesitate to tell you the experience was, and remains, the most difficult, painful thing we've ever gone through. Ever. It hurt like hell. It was scary. It was sad. It was dark.

We were afraid, but we weren't alone in that darkness. And in the midst of that suffocatingly difficult time, God was there. He gave us peace. He gave us hope. He gave us strength. And he continues to give us strength as we move forward, one day at a time. But, in addition, I believe through this experience he also gave us an assignment: to share this story and to walk this journey with you.

In that unspeakable pain, Jennie and I felt like God was gripping us with the greatness of his calling. He was telling us to share with people, not in spite of the difficult things they've gone through in this life, but in the midst of those things. Almost better *because* of the difficult things.

In the shock and grief at the hospital that night, after resuscitation failed, after the doctors told us they couldn't do anything more, we attempted to comprehend how we were supposed to simply drive away and leave her behind. As we sat in the car, frozen, my wife was hit with a realization. Jennie grabbed some invitation cards in the car and told me to go back into the hospital and invite those people to church for Christmas. "It's what Lenya would want you to do."

I was stunned. But she was right. Lenya loved to invite anyone and everyone to church, and she carried the invitation cards in her little purse. I took them from Jennie's hand and walked back into the emergency room. With tears streaming down my face, I approached the nurses' station and began handing them out. I pointed to the room where I had just left and said, "My little girl, whose body is right there behind that curtain, is in heaven with Jesus because she trusted in him. And in three days we're going to celebrate Jesus' birth into our world. In her honor, I would like to invite all of you to come. I'm supposed to be the one to speak, and I'm not quite sure how yet, but if you will come, I will preach."

In Lenya's honor, and because I didn't know what else to do, I kept the promise I made to the hospital employees and prepared to preach.

I'll never be able to escape the awfulness of those early days. Waking up and running to her empty room, panicking and delirious with grief, collapsing on her bed and holding her clothes to my chest. We somehow survived, though, and then came Christmas Eve.

I pulled out my sermon notes a few hours before the service and read what I had written. Immediately I sensed something was missing, and I knew exactly how to fix it.

Our family Christmas card was on the fireplace mantel. I opened it, looking at the beautiful pictures from the last time we posed for a photographer as a family of six, and found what I was looking for, what I desperately needed at that moment. On the last panel of the card, right above a shot of our six smiling faces was the text we had chosen, taken from 2 Timothy 1:10: "Jesus . . . has abolished death and brought life and immortality to light through the gospel."

I honestly don't know why we'd chosen that verse. It's a great verse and all, but it doesn't exactly taste like eggnog. It has Easter written all over it, but the vibe doesn't scream, "Happy birthday, Jesus!" Actually, Jennie and I had come across it during a Bible study in October, and we both bizarrely agreed it was a slam dunk for a Christmas card. So we sent it to the printers and thought no more about it.

But there was a problem at the printer. Delays stacked up, so they went out late. By the time they were mailed, they wouldn't hit homes until four days before Christmas. Our friends and supporters, who were hearing the heart-breaking news of Lenya's sudden and unexpected departure to heaven, would open their mailboxes that same afternoon to find happy, smiling photos of our family with the proclamation that "Jesus has abolished death and brought life and immortality to light through the gospel."

All of a sudden, the verse didn't seem like such an odd choice. It was perfect for this Christmas. Prophetic, even. Fitting for a holiday where our hearts were at half-mast. It was the message we needed to give and receive that day.

The truth is that death is what Christmas is all about. Jesus came to turn off the darkness of death by turning on the light. Hebrews 2:15 says Jesus came to release those "who through fear of death were all their lifetime subject to bondage." Christmas exists so there can be an Easter, so we can live with hope and die without fear.

This is the perspective I want to talk about. This is why we can rise above fear, pain, bondage, even death. He is turning off the dark all around us. And what we see in the light changes everything.

JESUS CAME TO TURN OFF THE DARKNESS OF DEATH BY TURNING ON THE LIGHT.

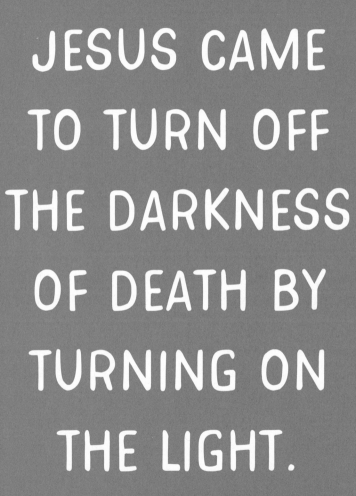

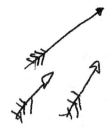

Prayer

Thank you, Father, that you've not only come to turn off the dark but offer peace in the process. Would you lift my eyes from fear and turn them to your face? Amen.

BREATHE, THINK, AND LIVE

x Every life is visited by darkness, and it is with great care I ask you to revisit yours. At what moments do you recall being stopped short by darkness or loss? What effect did it have on you?

x Can you discern how your calling in life may have been affected by this darkness or loss?

x What honest reactions do you have to the idea that suffering is not an obstacle to being used by God?

x What could it mean that your specific calling is not only unable to be stopped by darkness but may even be strengthened by it?

x What does it mean to you that Jesus has defeated death, our final enemy?

Day 9

||||| ||||

NOT FINISHED YET

 He too shared in their humanity so that by his death he might break the power of him who holds the power of death.

Hebrews 2:14 NIV

Here's something you need to know: hurting with hope still hurts. The sting of death might have been removed, but it still stings. It hurts like hell even when you know your loved one is in heaven.

I trust my daughter is "in a better place," as many are quick to remind me when they write encouraging notes—but that doesn't mean living without her is easy. I'm not going to sit here and tell you it was no big deal to have to face Christmas with our three daughters here on earth while Lenya's body was two miles away, lying in the funeral home that I still can't drive by without shaking and wanting to light myself on fire.

Even now, while the pain is not always unbearable, the weight hasn't gotten any lighter.

I have hope, but I'm not happy about it.

What I have discovered, though, is that neither is God.

God is not happy about it. He's furious. Not about hope but that we would need it. That we would have occasion for it. That's why he warned Adam and Eve in the garden to, at all costs, avoid the forbidden fruit (Genesis 2:17). He knew that sin would trigger death. He never intended for us to struggle in the surf, with wave after wave of sadness crashing down upon us—what Paul called "sorrow upon sorrow" (Philippians 2:27 KJV).

You see how Jesus really feels about grief and death in John 11. When confronted with the awfulness of the death of his friend Lazarus, and with sorrow upon sorrow playing in surround sound by Lazarus' sisters, Mary and Martha, he reacted viscerally. Jesus wept. He didn't hide his emotion or try to disguise his sadness. He didn't put sunglasses on or clumsily say, "It's okay! Lazarus has gone to a better place, everybody. He's probably playing football in my Father's house." No, he cried.

Even more shocking is what came next.

The Bible says twice that Jesus groaned in his spirit (John 11:33, 38). This was no ordinary sigh. The Greek word used here means "to bellow with rage." It is a word that is so strong it is normally used to describe the angry snorting of an agitated horse. You want to give a wide berth to an animal like that.

So much for gentle Jesus, meek and mild. He was fuming. Absolutely outraged. Mad at death. Angry at the grave, at sin, at the devil. But he wasn't just angry; he was angry enough to do something about it.

So what did Jesus do after raising Lazarus from the dead? He went on to defeat death in the most unlikely way ever—by dying.

Jesus used death, Satan's most powerful weapon, against him: "Through death He might destroy him who had the power of death, that is, the devil" (Hebrews 2:14).

But the power wasn't in dying; anyone can do that. Wait long enough, and it will happen to you. Jesus didn't just die—he rose from the dead. His soul reentered his decaying body and he got up! Unbelievably, he offers this same casket-exploding power to anyone who believes.

This is the gospel. Jesus has come and death has been stripped of its power. The dark has been switched off forever: "Having disarmed principalities and powers, He made a public spectacle of them, triumphing over them in it" (Colossians 2:15). He took the bullets out of the devil's gun. Satan can still pull the trigger, but there are only blanks inside. Instead of being terrified, we can actually look at death victoriously. This is what Paul meant when he said Jesus has abolished death.

But, you ask, why do we still have to die? For something that's been abolished, it seems as though business is booming. True, but remember this: God's not finished yet. The final destruction of death is still in the future. It hasn't happened yet, but it will. Not only will I see Lenya again, but I will hold the same body I held here, only better, because what the thief has stolen will be restored sevenfold (Proverbs 6:31)!

This is why it's crucial to remember that we don't need to put a nice face on our pain or hurry people through a process that can't be rushed: the fact that our sadness doesn't go away makes our triumph even more powerful. Our faith works in the fire, not just when life is fun. We can be hard-pressed and yet not crushed, struck down and yet not destroyed—not because we know general facts about the resurrection or that there is a heaven but because we trust in the one who said that he is the resurrection and the life. He took the keys from death and hell, was dead, and now lives forever. His name is Jesus, and he always leads us in triumph!

That Christmas Eve after Lenya went to heaven, it was time to make good on my commitment and speak.

It was incredibly emotional and overwhelming. I was a train wreck until moments before, alternately breaking down and feeling strong even while driving to the beautiful performing arts center we were using for the first of our services. During the worship portion of that first service, there were times when I doubted I would be able to stand up and walk to the platform, let alone make it through. But the moment I took the stage, I sensed the power of God, and I felt calm.

You can watch the message online, but I'll give you the highlights here. I had brought our Christmas card to the pulpit with me. After I preached that Jesus' birth signaled the end for loneliness, fear, despair, and guilt, I picked up the card and announced my final point. Looking at Lenya's face, I read the verse on the card and then declared that Jesus has turned off the darkness of death too. I told them what I want you and every human being on this planet to know: You don't have to fear death! It is defeated. Destroyed. It is painful, but there is no power left in it. In fact, for those who know Christ, death itself is a gift, for to be absent from the body is to be present with the Lord (2 Corinthians 5:8).

This is what God wants for you: forgiveness, a relationship with you, heaven.

OUR FAITH
WORKS IN
THE FIRE, NOT
JUST WHEN
LIFE IS FUN.

Though Christmas is Jesus' birthday, he offers you the present, the free gift of eternal life. Jesus left heaven and came to earth so we could go to heaven when we leave earth.

At the end of the message, I gave a simple invitation for people to stand and pray, to give their hearts to Jesus and receive that gift.

The Bible promises that if you believe in your heart that Jesus is Lord and confess with your mouth that he rose from the dead, you will be saved. You can pray something as simple as this: *God, I believe that I am a sinner. I'm broken, and I can't fix myself. I believe that Jesus is your Son and that he died on the cross in my place. I believe that he rose from the dead. I turn from my sins and turn to you. Please forgive me and help me follow you. In Jesus' name I pray, amen.*

A prayer that basic (or even more stripped down), if prayed in faith, has the power to change your heart and save your soul forever. In fact, you could say something like that to God right now as you're reading and be transformed from the inside out. If you never have, I pray that you will!

In response to that message, people from all of our campuses across the state of Montana stood and asked Jesus to turn off the dark in their hearts. Amazingly, there were also people who were watching our program on the internet and listening on the radio who decided to follow Jesus right where they were. What floored us was hearing later that among those who were present and moved that night were two paramedics who had attended in Lenya's honor.

Because of her, eyes were being opened to the reality of eternity. And through the lens of that reality, everything changes. God's not finished yet. Not by a mile.

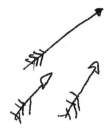

Prayer

Father, thank you for offering a faith that works in the fire and hope that holds in the storm. I choose to believe that you are using my life and my story to draw more people to your free gift of grace. Amen.

 BREATHE, THINK, AND LIVE

- x Does anything about Jesus' grief surprise you?
- x How does the fact that Jesus was angry enough to do something about death free us to feel our pain?
- x How has your fear of death manifested in your life? What about grief? How do people typically gloss over it in ways that aren't effective?
- x What about Jesus' attitude toward death could inform those reactions?
- x How does the fact that our sadness doesn't go away make our triumph more powerful?
- x Take a moment and reflect on what you believe about Jesus. Is there room for you to live deeper into the invitation he gives you?
- x How does the idea that God is not finished yet in abolishing death power us forward?

Day 10

|||| ||||

LENYA LENSES

 Jesus spoke to them, saying, "I am the light of the world. Whoever follows me will not walk in darkness, but will have the light of life."

John 8:12 ESV

Having my daughter go to heaven while I held her in my arms acted as a cataclysmic event, opening my eyes up to eternity like never before. It shook me from my cocoon of comfort and made the things of this world become visible and less desirable to me.

In *Strong Fathers, Strong Daughters*, Meg Meeker described parenting as "walking around with your heart outside your chest. It goes to school and gets made fun of. It jumps into cars that go too fast. It breaks and bleeds." Having my little girl leave this world made me long for the next one. It pulled my thoughts away from superficial things and took my mind behind the veil.

This is the goodness of grief, the grace of suffering. The flood of sorrow blasting its way through your soul wipes out attention previously devoted to trivial things. It's absolutely impossible to confront such powerful emotion and care about a Super Bowl commercial.

I found that grief undeniably enhanced my spiritual senses. Being so near to eternity causes you to almost be able to taste it. The unseen spiritual world becomes more vivid and more apparent than ever. There were moments, especially in the first few months after Lenya went to heaven, when I could sense the nearness of God's kingdom in a way that I had never in my life experienced before. God's whisper was amplified in the deafening roar of death and loss. I suppose that is what Jesus meant by, "Blessed are those who mourn" (Matthew 5:4 ESV). There are gifts you get from God in the midst of grief that you would never have had the bandwidth to receive if everything was going as planned. It was as though a lens that had been misaligned deep inside my soul was jolted into place now.

Without this lens, we can't see what's there. When we believe and see what God says is there, we are looking at it through the lens of faith. This corrected lens will change everything. We call it the Lenya lens. We've been seeing life through the eyes of Lenya Lion, who sees heaven every day. But we're not the only ones.

The night Lenya went to heaven, within a half hour of getting home, we received a call from the emergency room. When I answered the phone and heard it was someone from the hospital, my heart leaped. Maybe there had been a mix-up, and Lenya had just sat up. It was the opposite. The hospital was calling to ask whether we would be willing to donate Lenya's corneas and heart valves.

I wish I could say my reaction was noble, sacrificial, and generous. It wasn't. Everything in me coiled and stiffened, and I felt myself bristle. To think of doctors cutting into my daughter made me want to break something. But as Jennie and I talked and prayed about it, we thought about how Jesus was the first and ultimate organ donor. He donated his blood for us on the cross, and his righteousness was transplanted into our hearts.

Though we knew there was no wrong choice, we felt this was what God wanted us to do. To think that a part of our daughter might help someone physically see or enable someone to go through lifesaving surgery that could give them more time to come to know Jesus was just too beautiful of an opportunity to pass on.

Lenya was always extremely tender and compassionate. (I say *was* even though today she is more alive than she has ever been.) She had great instincts when it came to the well-being of those around her. She was constantly doing what she could to help cheer people up, which she usually accomplished by making them laugh. She was the official Lusko family court jester. Though it was and still is painful to think about, we made the decision to give these precious and costly gifts.

We were later notified that the transplants were successful. Today, there are two people on this earth to whom my daughter gave the gift of sight. They literally see life through Lenya Lion's eyes.

I have also been given the gift of sight. Having my daughter travel to the distant shores of heaven has opened my eyes to things unseen. I will walk with a limp, but I am better for it. I, too, look at life through different eyes. But it's not just a gift for me; it's a gift I desperately want to share with you.

After that lens snapped in, the things of this world grew strangely dim in the light of his glory and grace, as the old hymn puts it. While I can enjoy this world, I don't want it. I want something far greater. My soul cries out for what my daughter is experiencing. I long for the hidden treasures and secret pleasures that are in store for me in the presence of Jesus. There is still work to be done here, but deep down I can't wait for Jennie, Alivia, Daisy, Clover, Lennox, and me to all finish our races and go home.

Until that time, I want to keep that lens in place. To use it to focus in every day and see the invisible.

When the people who received Lenya's corneas got their Lenya lenses, what was scratched and cloudy and diseased became crystal clear. Disease was blocking the light from bouncing off the back of their corneas, but with her lenses, that was gone. The light could get in.

Jesus gives us new lenses. He is the light of the world that bounces off them and makes everything around us illuminated. Walking forward with his light in our eyes, we're going to see eternity. We're going to see the world differently. The dark won't stand a chance.

Prayer

Father, allow my pain and the circumstances of life to draw me closer to you and make me more aware of the nearness of heaven. When I don't know what to do, remind me to keep my eyes on you. Amen.

BREATHE, THINK, AND LIVE

- x In what way has loss hit you the hardest? Have you experienced God's goodness through the strangely wrapped present that is grief?
- x On what occasions have you longed for something greater than what this world offers? How does your heart cry out for heaven?
- x Thinking of eternity and heaven, do you perceive that anything has clouded your lenses? What keeps you from feeling heaven is near?
- x Do you think of heaven as a real place or struggle to grasp why it matters?
- x As a Christian, how can you move from the head knowledge that heaven is in the future toward the kind of knowledge that matters here and now? How can we allow it to make the things of earth seem dim?
- x How can our attitude toward heaven affect the work we still have to do here?

Day 11

HHt HHt I

BREAD AND CIRCUSES

So that we would not be outwitted by Satan;
for we are not ignorant of his designs.

2 Corinthians 2:11 ESV

Now that we have established the fact that you are special and destined for impact, that you are living in the present but made for eternity, it's time to recognize that, in addition, you've got a calling. But know this: God's not the only one who knows you're special and specially called. Your Enemy knows it too, and he is desperate to keep you from realizing it and reaching your potential.

Our new lenses enable us to see eternity and what's happening in the invisible around us. But they wouldn't be doing their job if they didn't also show us what's happening on the other side, where darkness rules.

Paul said that we should not be ignorant of Satan's devices (2 Corinthians

2:11). That means we open our eyes to his ways and his weapons. We get wise to the invisible war being waged all around us, and we learn to spot attacks.

God's Word tells us what our Enemy is like. Jesus said that he is the father of lies and that there isn't a shred of truth in him (John 8:44). In other words, the way you can tell that the devil is lying is if his lips are moving. Nothing he says can be trusted. Scripture also tells us that he "walks about like a roaring lion, seeking whom he may devour" (1 Peter 5:8). He's super dangerous too. He won't even show up except to steal, to kill, and to destroy (John 10:10). And get this: he really hates you. A lot. He's out to get you.

What's his problem?

He's going to hell.

God promised way back in the garden of Eden that the devil is going down. He will be swiftly crushed under our feet (Romans 16:20). There's nothing he can do about it, and he knows it. He doesn't want to go down empty-handed, though, for misery loves company. Since he can't stop God from throwing him into hell, he will try to hurt God by taking as many of the people God loves with him when he goes.

It's similar to what happens at pool parties when people get thrown into the water. They hold on to things for as long as they can to try to keep from being thrown in, but then their strategy changes when they realize it's inevitable. *If I'm going in, I'm bringing you all with me* is the prevailing thinking. That, coupled with a narcissistic god complex, just about sums up Satan's MO.

We are just pawns to the devil. He knows that we matter to God, though, and since he can't hurt God directly, he inflicts pain on him indirectly by hurting us. If you have put your faith in Jesus, Satan can't pluck you out of God's hand.

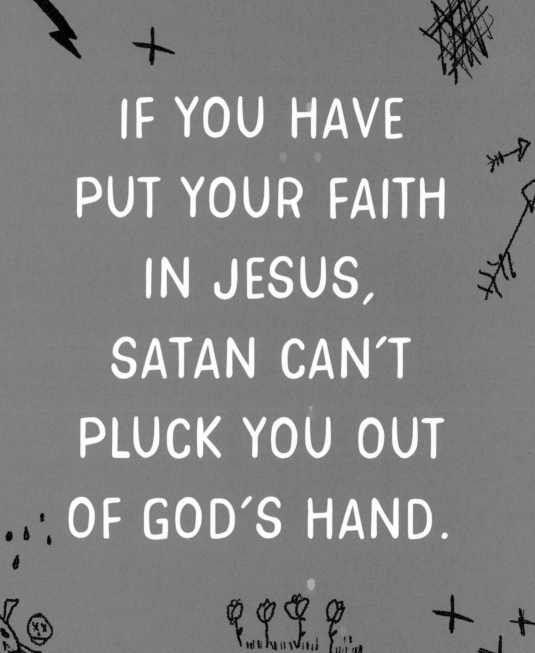

IF YOU HAVE PUT YOUR FAITH IN JESUS, SATAN CAN'T PLUCK YOU OUT OF GOD'S HAND.

While we are no match for Satan, he is no match for God. Greater is he who is in us than he who is in the world (1 John 4:4). Satan might be like a lion—I think he's more of a hyena—but Jesus is the Lion of the tribe of Judah, the true King of the jungle. Satan would love for you to think he is all-powerful. He's not. He has to ask God for permission to mess with us. God has also established limits to temptation so that there is always a way to escape.

You can see this illustrated in the wilderness temptation of Jesus, when Satan stood behind Jesus and told him to jump off the temple (Matthew 4:5–6). Why would the devil tell Jesus to jump? Because he couldn't push him! I guarantee that if he could have, he would have. He could only whisper in Jesus' ear, not make him do it.

So it is when Satan comes your way with his bag of tricks. He doesn't want you to know this, but he can't make you do anything. *You always have a choice.* In that way, you are more dangerous to yourself than the devil is. He has to check with God before he can wreak havoc in your life, but you can do great damage to your calling without getting approval from anyone.

Our biggest mistake in this war is that we often underestimate our Enemy's creativity. We think he is only capable of surprise attacks, like a breaching great white shark. By default, when I think about Satan attacking, in my head I hear the *Jaws* theme song. An antagonistic coworker goes out of his way to make you look bad and lies about you for nothing other than your faith. A friend at school mocks you when she finds out you are a virgin and pressures you to get some action. Someone breaks into your house and robs you while you are on a mission trip. Outright attack is certainly an effective strategy that the devil does employ, but it is not his only trick.

Sticks and stones aren't the only weapons in his arsenal. He often resorts to something much more dangerous, something I call *panem et circenses*. Wikipedia that if you want, but I'll save you the time. It's Latin for "bread and circuses," and it's part of a quote from a Roman writer named Juvenal, from around AD 100: "For the People who once upon a time handed out military command, high civil office, legions—everything, now restrains itself and anxiously hopes for just two things: bread and circuses."

This ancient dude was describing the way the people of the Roman Empire had been tricked into giving up their freedom as citizens. They allowed the emperors to take away their power to vote, elect their own officials, and govern themselves. These priceless things had been purchased on the cheap. All it had taken was grain and games. Food and entertainment. Bread and circuses.

During the imperial age, under Julius Caesar, Augustus, Tiberius, Caligula, Claudius, Nero, and their successors, as many as 135 days out of the year were dedicated to games: gladiator matches, chariot races, juggling competitions, and elaborate entertainments. These emperors found that as long as people weren't hungry or bored, their freedom could be stolen. In the process, the emperors could turn themselves from kings into gods. The free food and endless entertainment acted as an anesthetic. They kept people amused while their liberty was taken. It was poison laced with sugar, and it was incredibly effective. The people shortsightedly gave up things that mattered for things that were over in a short period of time.

The devil is all over bread and circuses. It's his favorite. He wants you to give up what Christ died for you to have, and he knows that if he can distract you, he can destroy you.

This destruction by distraction is difficult to detect when it's happening, because it doesn't involve bad things but good things that take the place of the most important things.

You do not have to fall for Satan's tricks. Open your eyes! Use your lenses! Life is more than who's fighting whom in UFC, what so-and-so tweeted, which celebrities just broke up, and what the latest and greatest food truck is serving up. You were meant to live on a higher level.

When your life is focused on the superficial, you can be kept from your calling and deprived of your destiny. The Enemy's end game is to play the fiddle while the life you were meant to live goes up in smoke.

Don't mistake what I'm saying. There's nothing wrong with food or fun. Football, wine, cycling, travel, Twitter, and fashion. These are all good things God wants us to enjoy while we are on earth. I'm convinced that he takes pleasure as we enjoy our lives. He smiles as we eat and laugh, run and play. But these things, in and of themselves, aren't enough. We were never supposed to live our lives purely on the physical playing field. We were meant for so much more.

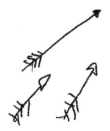

Prayer

Father, give me strength for the wilderness and wisdom in the face of temptation. Keep me from distraction so I can keep my eyes on what truly matters—the best thing. Amen.

BREATHE, THINK, AND LIVE

× Does the fact that you have an enemy targeting you freak you out or light a fire under you? Why? How so?

× What causes us to be ignorant of Satan's devices?

× Have you seen the Enemy act in your life? How so? How did you know?

× How does keeping our lenses on, looking toward eternity and heaven, place us in relation to our Enemy?

× Have you ever heard the excuse "the devil made me do it" (literally or in essence)? How does the fact that the devil can't make you, as a child of God, do anything actually free you to deal with the real problems?

× Look, we've all fallen for the "bread and circuses" trap. How do you most commonly fall for it in your daily life? What are you handing over when you choose an anesthetic over what is real and eternal?

× How can we keep good things from becoming distractions? What does it mean to live on a higher level?

Day 12

HHT HHT II

THE HARM OF BEING A HYBRID

 Our citizenship is in heaven, and from it we await a Savior, the Lord Jesus Christ.

Philippians 3:20 ESV

In the 1990s a breeding experiment between Asiatic and African lions in India went horribly wrong. Scientists tried to mix the two together, but it backfired. The hybrid lions' back legs were too weak to support them. Some were so feeble they couldn't even eat meat off the bone and had to be served boneless meat.

There were originally about eighty of these hybrids, a figure that was down to twenty-one when I read about it. They are kept in a small enclosure, nicknamed the "old age home" for lions. Those who take care of them are basically just waiting for them to die. The photos of these pitiful creatures were heartbreaking. One reporter noted that the lions "are extremely weak. They can barely stand up or walk. Their only activity is a small but painful walk to eat their meals. However, if challenged, they can still muster a spine-chilling roar."

This sad story is a picture of what is at stake if you don't fight to keep your heart set on heaven. The Enemy wants to clip your wings and declaw your calling. If he can get you to mix enough compromise into your life, he will slowly be able to slip a muzzle over your snout. You are meant to live a life that's not laced but totally offered up to God as a living sacrifice.

Too many Christians are tricked out of their power through their purity being diluted and their perspective being grounded. So let's unground that perspective, shall we?

In Philippians 3:19, Paul said that we are not to focus only on earthly things, for to live that way is to have your belly as your god, worshipping your body and focusing on only what you can eat, drink, and touch. Life is more than eating and the body more than what you wear (Matthew 6:25). Plus, Paul said, to live focused on things of the earth doesn't make sense for a Christian, because our citizenship is in heaven (Philippians 3:20).

This would have immediately fired off bells for the Philippians he was writing to. The city of Philippi was a Roman colony. And unlike neighboring cities, those who lived in Philippi enjoyed Roman citizenship, which was a really big deal.

The majority of those in Philippi had never set foot in Rome, but they were under its protection and its privileges. In the annals of Rome their names were recorded. Though they were far from Rome, it was technically their home. They lived in Philippi, but their citizenship was somewhere else.

As a Christian, the same is true for you. You live here, but heaven is your home country. If you have put your faith in Christ, this world is no longer your home. You live in it but are not of it. You are just passing through. Your time here is just a long layover. Your current status is resident alien.

That's not just some nice thought or wishful thinking. There's a paper trail to back it up.

You see, both birth and death are citizenship-altering events. You become a citizen when you are born. The government gives you a certificate of live birth and a Social Security card, and you can get a passport, a driver's license, and so on. When you die there's paperwork too. The government sends a death certificate in the mail.

I'll never forget the day I opened up the envelope that contained Lenya's death certificate. It came exactly twenty days after she went to heaven. It was the harshest letter I've ever opened.

I was working through a stack of mail, and opening it up was like stepping on a land mine. Seeing her beautiful name on such a ghastly document was crushing. I held it in my hands and shook with sadness.

In God's grace, the next envelope I opened was from a friend, who enclosed a $50,000 check made out to our church, with Lenya's name on the memo line. His desire was for us to turn off the dark and see God make the devil pay in her honor. I felt the Lord once again calling me to channel my anger and sadness to turn the pain into seeds that could be planted and produce a harvest.

The death certificate we received that day ended my daughter's citizenship in this country. She is no longer an American. When census takers count up the total number of citizens of the United States, they don't include Abraham Lincoln. He is not a citizen anymore either.

Salvation affects spiritual citizenship because it is an event that encompasses both birth and death. Being born again is dying: to sin, to your old life, to this world. And it's birth: new life in Christ is planted inside your chest. Just as

Christ rose from the dead, you are raised to walk in newness of life. Colossians 3:3 says, "For you have died, and your life is hidden with Christ in God" (ESV).

Where's the paperwork for this spiritual death and birth? It was nailed to the cross. At the moment you believed, your citizenship in this world was canceled. You were transferred out of the kingdom of darkness and into the kingdom of light. And there's paperwork done for this part too. Your name is written in the Book of Life (Philippians 4:3; Luke 10:20).

From that moment on, you live in this world, but you are not of this world. You are a part of an entirely different kingdom.

Still, the gravitational pull of this world is constant and disorienting. Interference gets in the way of heaven's homing signal at every turn. We can be lulled into a false sense of home, but in the end, we have no choice but to leave.

We can't focus on heaven and on the distractions of this world at the same time. We are not meant to be a hybrid of those two kinds of lions. Refuse to live a life that is muzzled. You weren't meant to hobble back and forth between Jesus and the world, a sickly hybrid version of the person you were born to be.

Instead, with the tips of your toes on the edge of eternity, fix your eyes on the true Lion, and you'll see through the lies of the Enemy.

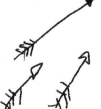

Prayer

Thank you, Father, for saving a seat for me in heavenly places and paving a way for me to be with you. Make dull the pull of this world and realign my heart with heaven. Amen.

BREATHE, THINK, AND LIVE

- Have you ever felt like a weaker hybrid between the world and Jesus or like you were less effective because you were trying to play both fields? What caused you to feel this way? What did you lose in the process?
- How do you see a culture around us that has its belly as its god? What is the most common way this comes up in your daily life and interactions?
- What's it like to be in a place where you aren't a citizen? If you've experienced this or know others who have, how might that affect your choices and actions?
- If you've been issued a death certificate for this world and a birth certificate for the next, how does that change your identity?
- Practically, what does it mean for you to be in but not of the world?
- When do you feel a false sense of home? What kinds of things make you uneasy, like you belong elsewhere?

Day 13

$$\text{卌 卌 |||}$$

PAIN IS A MICROPHONE

 No one should be shaken by these afflictions; for you yourselves know that we are appointed to this.

1 Thessalonians 3:3

What would William Wallace be without the heartbreaking loss of his wife? Just another guy in a kilt. It was the occasion of his great suffering that turned him into Braveheart and thrust him onto the platform of not only national attention in his day but also has kept him alive in mythical proportions today. Anguish has the capacity to turn up the volume on a life. Pain is a microphone, and the more it hurts the louder you get.

Pain is guaranteed. The Bible says the rain falls on the evil and the good alike (Matthew 5:45). Part of living on this fallen planet cursed by sin is that trials are inherent. That's just the way it is. Pain comes with the territory.

Actually, as a child of God, difficulties often ramp up to a whole other level. Why? Because as the great theologian Spider-Man said, "With great power comes great responsibility."

The Enemy of your soul is not going to let you capture his flag without some serious flak. When you stand up as a Christian, attempt to share your faith, and live to see lost people won, you'll invite suffering, persecution, and opposition your way. This is why Paul told Timothy, "All who desire to live godly in Christ Jesus will suffer persecution" (2 Timothy 3:12).

But be of good cheer. There is a connection between the strength of our pain and the volume of our voices. The more we hurt, the louder we become. The things God deposits in your spirit in the midst of suffering are the same things that someday other people will desperately need.

There are two reasons why your volume gets louder as life gets harder. First, when you're going through a great time of trial, people around you tend to get quieter. Their voices hush out of respect. Smart people walk on tiptoe around hearts that are on fire.

When you're a Christian and you're going through a great time of difficulty, you will notice that those around you who don't know Jesus Christ—especially those you've shared your faith with before—will lean in extra close. You told them that Jesus is the light of your world. Well, now your power has been cut, and they want to see if you can glow in the dark. If they do see your claims proven true, you'll find a greater willingness on their part to trust Christ in their own lives.

The second reason your volume gets louder when life get harder is because, during trials, you can hear God better. Why is this? Because he comes closer!

That's what we find in Psalm 34:18: "The LORD is near to those who have a broken heart."

C. S. Lewis wrote, "God whispers to us in our pleasures, speaks in our conscience, but shouts in our pain; it is His megaphone to rouse a deaf world." And the nearer he is, the better we can hear him and the more we can do for him.

You're actually better fit for ministry in the crucible of pain, when you've faced or are facing darkness. It's counterintuitive, but in the middle of my hardest mess, I had a greater desire than ever before to tell the whole world that Jesus Christ can turn off the dark because I experienced it myself. Jennie and I found that when we poured our pain into ministry, whole new levels of usefulness opened up. There's perhaps no time you are as powerful as when you minister in the midst of pain.

Plus, hard times are a passport that gives you permission to go places you wouldn't get to any other way. Pain can open doors that would otherwise remain locked. There are avenues of influence. There are situations and opportunities you will stumble upon that would never have been yours had things gone well. People you never would have met had you not been to chemotherapy, a doctor's visit, or a trip to yet another rehab facility to pick up your son.

Jesus articulated this perfectly in John 12:24, when he said, "Most assuredly, I say to you, unless a grain of wheat falls into the ground and dies, it remains alone; but if it dies, it produces much grain." Think about it: going into the ground and dying is not great for the grain. It's a bummer. But the difficulty causes what emerges from the ground to be wonderful.

I told you earlier about how Jennie told me to invite the people who

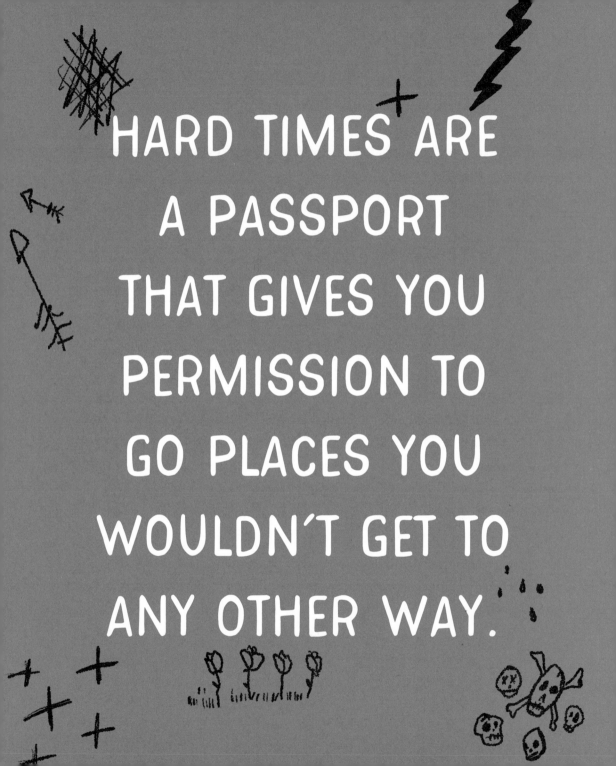

HARD TIMES ARE A PASSPORT THAT GIVES YOU PERMISSION TO GO PLACES YOU WOULDN'T GET TO ANY OTHER WAY.

worked in the emergency room to come to church on Christmas Eve. She saw what I hadn't. The microphone called pain was waiting to be seized. Later, we received a note at our church from a respiratory therapist I invited, a woman who was married to the doctor who had tried to resuscitate Lenya and had told us he was unable to do anything more. She wasn't exactly comfortable going to church, but she wanted to come as a tribute to Lenya. This is what she wrote:

> Levi's words went through my whole body . . . in and out. So many questions were answered. I have never felt so good about listening to someone speak of the Lord before. I just stared at him preaching, and I felt comfortable. I am still thinking in my head how I understand life and death more now than I ever have before. Before it was more on the medical side. People pass on, but kids should not. Now I am able to understand and feel semi-okay with a child leaving earth and going to heaven. I have never felt that before. I feel a bit ashamed, maybe even lost as in my youth and not understanding where my faith really was. Levi's words laid it out for me. I finally understood so many things I thought I never would.

Not every opportunity to minister through pain will be so direct, and many times we will not know the outcome until we get to heaven. I never would have walked into a hospital that night to invite strangers to come to church, but my pain became a passport into that place. I dare you to look at the hardships you're facing and believe that, through them, there are people you are meant to reach.

Remember, God doesn't cause bad things to happen, but he is sovereign, and nothing happens outside his permission. The devil is the one ultimately responsible for evil. Sometimes it seems that life is out of control and more is given to us than we can bear. But everything is under God's control, and he leads us to break through when we worship, no matter what we're going through. His end game is to sabotage all your suffering and use what was meant for evil to accomplish his purposes. He has the devil's credit card number on file and is more than able to make him pay for the damage he does.

So actively be on the lookout for every way you can redeem the hell you are put through by shining your light in the darkness. Let nothing be wasted. Hold nothing back. None of your tears have fallen to the ground unseen. God has a plan to put each of your difficulties to use like a seed that goes into the ground and brings forth a harvest of righteousness.

I also want you to believe in Jesus' name that there will come a day when the devil will regret ever asking God's permission to give you your trials, because you will end up twice as blessed as you started out. God's up to something! He's turning your mess into a message. He's turning your pain into a platform. He's turning your trial into a testimony. He's turning the trash that has come into your life into triumph!

I have a prayer for you. Whether you've lost a job, whether you've lost a relationship, whether you had a dream that you believed was going to come to pass and it seems to have fizzled to nothing under your nose, my prayer for all the grief you've gone through is that God would help you to see that there is power in the pain. Suffering is not an obstacle to being used by God; it's an opportunity to be used like never before. Your calling still stands.

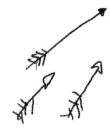

Prayer

Father, help me to not waste my pain. Remind me in the face of my most difficult days that you are working in my circumstances and turning my mess into a message. Amen.

 BREATHE, THINK, AND LIVE

- × Has anyone ever given you a gift by sharing their painful experience? Walked you through something? Lent support? (This could be someone you know personally or someone in the public sphere.) How was that a gift to you?
- × Has your personal pain ever positioned you to influence others? How can you or have you shared it in a way that lifts others up?
- × What places have you gained access to through circumstances you wouldn't have asked for and wouldn't otherwise have come near?
- × Who might be listening closer if you were to open up and share your experience of God through your pain? Why is that?
- × If you're a grain of wheat that has to be crushed to grow, what beautiful thing might be growing out of the husk of the past?

Day 14

||||| ||||| ||||

THE WAR ON DARKNESS

Set your mind on things above, not
on things on the earth.

Colossians 3:2

Jesus turned off the dark, vanquished death, and gave us citizenship in heaven. He gave us lenses to see the invisible and a microphone in our pain. And he has made us a light in this dark world.

Here's where we get dangerous. Now that Jesus has turned off the dark eternally, we get to join him in turning it off here on earth. Now that we see with spiritual eyes, we get to declare war on the darkness in all its forms—wherever it occurs, either outside us or inside us.

I have no doubt the devil sends demons to mess with me. The world might very well be another source of problems that come at me. But this I know for sure: I cause more than enough problems to keep myself occupied.

No matter where problems are coming from, I've made a decision. I declare war. On darkness. On my demons. On anxiety and succumbing to the nights of the black dog of depression. On my self-sabotaging tendencies. My selfishness. My narcissism and the way I can spend hours doing nothing when I should be focusing on only one thing.

I declare war on darkness.

I am not asking you to help me fight my battles, but I want to do everything I can to convince you to engage with yours.

Give it a try. Say "I declare war."

There is freedom in this declaration.

You can't win a conflict you don't admit you are in. Declaring war separates you from the problems that you can so easily mistake for permanent parts of your identity and distances you from your thoughts, your fears, and your anxieties. You are not your darkness. You are not your dysfunctional behavior or the pain that has invaded your life uninvited. You are not your overeating or your obsessive TV watching or your judgmental, critical comments you wish didn't keep coming out of your mouth. You are not your mistakes or your transgressions or what you see in your dark and twisted dreams. Choosing to oppose those things is to make it clear that they are not on your side. This is the only way to get out of your rut and move past them.

When you choose to declare war, you are refusing to go gently in the night

YOU CAN'T WIN A CONFLICT YOU DON'T ADMIT YOU ARE IN.

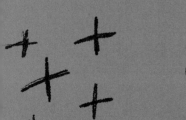

or to be taken without a fight. You are declaring war on the version of yourself that you don't want to be. You're choosing a different direction.

You don't turn off darkness by yelling at it, waving it away, or willing it to be gone. You walk across the room and flip the light switch. Or you ask Alexa to turn the lights on.

Never look where you don't want to go. Don't focus on what you don't want to think about. Instead, direct your thoughts to a better destination. This is what Paul meant when he wrote, "Set your mind on things above, not on things on the earth" (Colossians 3:2).

Begin with your thoughts. Turn off the dark there.

My friend Kevin Gerald likes to say, "Thoughts are like trains: they take you somewhere." When a train of thought shows up, don't just get on! Slow down before you board it to make sure it's heading in the right direction. Ask each one: *Where are you taking me? Are we headed to Lovelyville, Virtuetown, Good Report Station? Boomsauce! Wait, this train is going to Jealousy, USA? Rage City? Gossip Central? I'm sorry, I'm just not comfortable going where you are headed.*

This is an obvious strategy when you're staring down a dark thought. Thoughts of murder, for example, can pretty quickly be spotted as trains you don't want to get on. But you can also avoid boarding trains like these:

- *You'll never top this success. You've peaked.*
- *. You'll never escape your past.*
- *You'll never achieve your dreams.*
- *You'll never make it out of this alive.*

- *You don't have what it takes.*
- *You won't get to see your kids grow up.*
- *You're defined by the difficult things you have been through.*
- *You don't deserve anything good.*
- *Nobody loves you and you should just die.*

Sometimes, though, it's harder to spot trains headed to negative destinations. Watch out for thoughts like these:

- Being suspicious of people's motives
- Wondering what went wrong
- Feeling guilty
- Doubting and questioning God
- Worrying
- Obsessing about why you weren't invited
- Fearing someone you love being harmed
- Secretly being happy when something bad happens to someone you don't like
- Stressing about your future
- Stewing over something that was done to you

The point is this: you have a choice.

You can avoid a train that's headed to a dangerous destination by not boarding it in the first place. What do you do when you identify a thought that doesn't pass inspection? The same thing TSA would do to you if the X-ray machine showed a weapon in your carry-on: You take it captive. Detain it. Don't let it into your mind for a minute. Show it no mercy. Give it no quarter. Send that thought to the pit of despair so the six-fingered man and the albino can torture it.

Don't be kind. Remember, this is war.

Maybe you've found that you can't stop thinking about something by trying to stop thinking about it. The only way to guarantee you'll keep thinking about Dwight Schrute is to try to stop thinking about Dwight Schrute. So instead of stopping a thought, replace a thought. You have to actively feed the positive and starve the negative.

How do we do this?

I've found the best way is through reciting Scripture and singing worship songs. Paul also pointed to the power of this strategy: "Let the word of Christ dwell in you richly in all wisdom, teaching and admonishing one another in psalms and hymns and spiritual songs, singing with grace in your hearts to the Lord" (Colossians 3:16). Scripture puts your mind and heart into an airplane mode that makes it impervious to low-living, low-thinking communication that we are so often bombarded by.

I've included some of my favorite verses in the back of this book. I encourage you to look through them. Memorize your favorites. Whenever a thought doesn't pass inspection, use one of the verses to evict that thought.

These are just some of the weapons we have to fight in this war. On the rest of this journey, we're going to discover that we have a lot of firepower. Not only do we have lenses that give us spiritual eyes to see what's going on around us, but we have the backing to do something about it. So declare war. Get out of your own way and step into the life you were born to live.

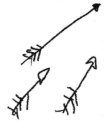

Prayer

Father, give me a steely resolve in the face of conflict, dysfunction, and self-sabotaging tendencies. Give me strength for the fight and courage to declare war. Amen.

BREATHE, THINK, AND LIVE

- ✗ What part of darkness, personal or general, are you absolutely fed up with?
- ✗ What would it mean for you to declare war on that thing? On darkness in general?
- ✗ Knowing Jesus has already defeated darkness in an eternal sense, how does that empower you to participate in turning it off around you?
- ✗ Let's look inside your head. If your thoughts are like trains, where would they be taking you?
- ✗ Do you find yourself looking where you don't want to go in terms of your thought life? List three places where that happens.
- ✗ In those places, how can you avoid getting on the train in the first place?
- ✗ What thought will you replace it with?

x Seek out a scripture that addresses these trains you don't want to get on and memorize it. Look for worship songs to sing or a prayer you can repeat when those trains pull up to your station.

x What excites you about declaring war? What worries you? Talk about these things with God and keep them in mind as we move forward.

WEEK 3

CROSS THE BARBED WIRE

Day 15

HHT HHT HHT

OVER THE LINE

 Be strong and courageous, and do the work. Do not be afraid or discouraged, for the Lᴏʀᴅ God, my God, is with you. He will not fail you or forsake you.

1 Chronicles 28:20 ɴɪᴠ

When you decide you're done being pushed around by darkness in your life, and you're ready to become a victor, you will find that a wolf rises in your heart.

That is how Theodore Roosevelt, the youngest person to hold the office of president, described the "power of joy in battle" that floods a person who chooses to meet the challenge spread out before him. This larger-than-life president, who is literally chiseled in stone on Mount Rushmore (and is permanently one and the same with Robin Williams because of *Night at the Museum*, at least in my mind), led the Rough Riders on horseback into the battle for San Juan Hill during the Spanish-American War. Machine gun bullets sprayed out from the top of the mountain, cutting down man after man, yet Teddy fought on, relentlessly urging his men forward.

In that terrible situation he crossed a barbed-wire fence that lay across the battlefield. That was the moment. That's when he fully committed to the action before him, and at that moment a wolf rose in his heart. With his trademark spectacles fogged from the humidity and a handkerchief trailing from the back of his sombrero, he steeled himself. He gave no thought to the bullets flying all around him as he urged forward his horse, Little Texas. Teddy had flipped a switch inside, and he was unstoppable in his resolve to do what was necessary. A witness said that from the instant TR stepped across the wire, he "became the most magnificent soldier I have ever seen." A shell exploded near him, burning his skin, yet he pressed on. A stray bullet nicked his elbow, but he didn't notice. He didn't stop until the battle was won. For the rest of his life, he referred to that day, July 1, 1898, as the greatest day of his life. The day the wolf rose in his heart.

"Wait a minute," I hear you say. "Why would I want to rise up like a wolf? You, me, and little Red Riding Hood all know wolves aren't a good time." Only in fairy tales. Consider this: Wolves were created by God and are truly remarkable creatures known for loyalty and strength. In addition to being highly social and smart, they also have other lesser-known qualities you should want in your life. These ferocious hunters also willingly play the part of foster parents. A wolf is not just to be a brave warrior; it is also to be a loving nurturer, and that is what we've all been called to.

"Okay, then what does the barbed-wire fence represent?" Consider the barbed wire to be the separation of the man that he was and the man he knew he needed to be in the moment. Think what he was facing. The enemy was pelting him and his men with bullets from a high point. They had the advantage. People were being cut down. With death all around him, amid danger and fear, he caught sight of that wire fence. And he drew the line inside himself. He made the decision to not turn back but instead to press forward like he knew he needed to. And as he did, he became this magnificent soldier, this relentless force. And he prevailed.

On our battlefields in this war we fight, we'll meet up with our own barbed-wire fence. We'll get the opportunity to rise like a wolf. When we look at what's happening inside us, we'll stare down the separation between who we are and who we need to be. Bullets will be flying, but we'll steel ourselves. And we'll make the decision to cross the barbed wire.

There is incredible power in setting all that is within you in a singular direction. So much of the time we defensively react to what comes our way. It's time to *stop letting life happen to you and start happening to your life*. Meet the enemy on your terms, even if that enemy is you. Go on the offensive. Whether you are a sophomore in college or you are in your sixties and contemplating life after retirement, when you decide to stare the things in the face that are holding you back, strength will bubble up inside your chest.

As twentieth-century Scottish explorer W. H. Murray wrote, "The moment one definitely commits oneself, then Providence moves too . . . raising in one's favour all manner of unforeseen incidents and meetings and material assistance, which no man could have dreamed would have come his way."

Declare war and the wolf will rise.

In the coming week, we're going to stare down three fields of battle: how

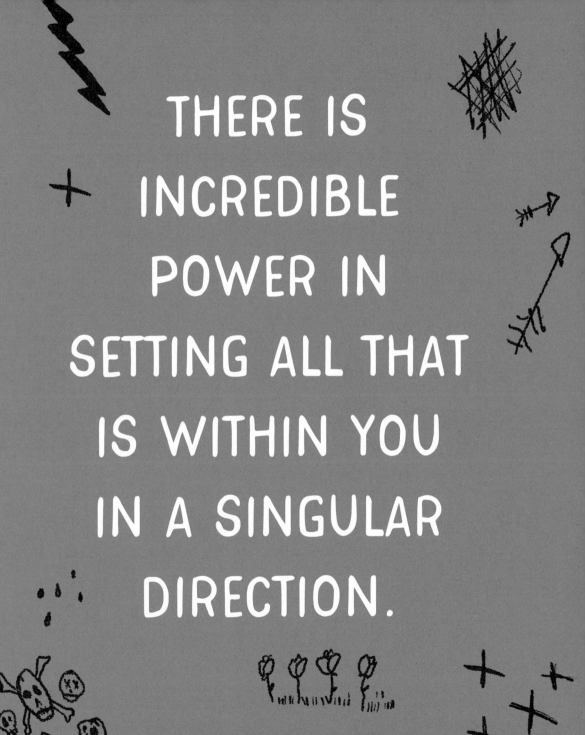

THERE IS INCREDIBLE POWER IN SETTING ALL THAT IS WITHIN YOU IN A SINGULAR DIRECTION.

you think, how you speak, and how you act. We're going to approach a turning point in each of those key areas, and I know that you'll cross it bravely.

But don't freak out. Stay away from WebMD. You're not going to have to face this by yourself or fight alone. You have an enormous amount of backup and firepower at your disposal. I'll tell you all about it.

Next in this journey, we'll talk about the keys to winning the battle within yourself.

I have lived the principles I'm going to share with you. They're at play in my life right now, every single day. But I finally crossed the barbed wire because I know you need these concepts as much as I do.

So let's make it official. We've talked about declaring war, but now I want you to write down your declaration of war. In what ways do you need to get out of your own way? Don't sanitize your list. The time for half measures is over. To be clean, you must come clean.

I think that if you make the decision to go forward where you feel like shirking back, if you cross that barbed wire, you'll find that power rising in you.

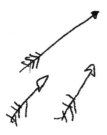

Prayer

Father, humble me to see the areas I'm weak, the speech that needs attention, the thoughts that need rerouting, and the words that need softening. I want to be changed by you. Make me kind. Amen.

BREATHE, THINK, AND LIVE

Write down your declaration of war here:

The Things Holding Me Back

I DECLARE WAR

On this day _____

At this time _____

Signed _____

x What's the difference between the person you are now and the person you need to be as you come to your own barbed wire in this war?

x How would you describe the person you need to be? What bullets are coming at you?

x What areas of your thoughts, words, or habits are not in line with that person you need to be?

x For Teddy Roosevelt, it was either muster that wolf within or lose the fight, possibly his life, and the lives of his men. Can you see how you're also facing the same kind of urgency as you battle the things that keep you from living the life God has for you?

x Thinking with eternal lenses as we did last week, with all its great cosmic implications, how important is making that critical move across the barbed wire?

x What are you hoping will be different about you after this process?

Day 16

HHT HHT HHT I

A HOSTAGE SITUATION

Because of the Lord's great love we are not consumed,
for his compassions never fail.
They are new every morning;
great is your faithfulness.

Lamentations 3:22–23 NIV

In Las Vegas, the escalators and moving sidewalks seem to move in only one direction: toward the casinos. Getting in is as easy as finding a Ding Dong at a truck stop. On the other hand, finding your way out is, by design, much more difficult. The intention is to trap you in a maze of distraction that will cause you to spend as much time and money as possible.

When I find myself battling with moodiness, I feel as though I'm being carried along on a moving sidewalk, headed to a place I won't like and that I'll have a hard time finding my way back from. Moodiness is a trap, but it's one we can escape, even if it seems ingrained.

I started experiencing this sensation in high school. Something would happen to set me off: feeling excluded, being made fun of, embarrassing myself with something I said or did. The next thing I knew, I felt like the ground was moving under my feet.

I was officially in a bad mood. Well, some people call it a bad mood. I call it being held hostage by the version of me I don't want to be. You can rearrange my name to spell *evil*, so I call him *Evilevi*. He might have my fingerprints and blood type, but he is no friend of mine.

Whether it set in after lunch, during second period, or in the car on the way to school, once I was in it, I was in it. A wall went up, and my enjoyment of life went down. It's impossible to be at ease when you're clenched up on the inside. After an hour or two, whatever originally set me off was no longer the issue; self-pity and self-loathing were the real problems. Eventually I'd give up on the entire day. I'd get to a place where I'd think, *This day is spoiled. I'll just have to try again tomorrow.*

You've felt that way, haven't you? *Tomorrow is a new day. This one's no good.* We do the same thing when we've made a bad choice about eating: *I fell off the wagon for lunch, so I might as well binge at dinner and have a cupcake at bedtime. I should have had a healthy breakfast, but since I didn't, the whole day is shot. I'll do better on Monday . . . or next month.*

Where did we get the idea that one bad decision must be followed by another? Maybe it comes from failing to understand the true meaning of an often-quoted verse written by the prophet Jeremiah in the book of

Lamentations: "Because of the LORD's great love we are not consumed, for his compassions never fail. They are new every morning; great is your faithfulness" (3:22–23 NIV).

Jeremiah *isn't* saying a new morning is the only time you have the opportunity to receive mercy; there isn't anything mystical attached to the clock striking midnight. That's not when God's mercies replenish. Your AT&T data plan might roll over at a specific time, but that's not so with the devotion God has allocated for you.

Rather, you always have a new shot because God is that good. You have the option to go to him morning, noon, and night—once a day, nine times a day, every hour if you need to—and claim the help you need for the present struggle you are facing. Hebrews 4:16 says, "So let us boldly approach God's throne of grace. Then we will receive mercy. We will find grace to help us when we need it" (NIRV). You don't have to wait for the start of day; you can seek the grace *when you need it.*

You needn't write off a day that has been tainted. You can start over on the spot. Shake your internal Etch A Sketch! There are brand-new mercies waiting for you. Only pride and silliness allow a bad decision to turn into a bad day and make you defer until tomorrow what you need to do right now.

The truth is this: you don't have to stay in a bad mood any more than you have to stay in the wrong Uber. If you got in, you can get out. A bad mood exists only in your mind. That's why any discussion of taking back your life has to start with talking about your mind. You can't live right if you won't think right.

I've learned a lot about what makes me tick, but I still struggle to control my mood. Simply put, *my ability to respond well to external battles has everything to do with my ability to fight the internal war successfully.*

Proverbs 25:28 tells us, "Whoever has no rule over his own spirit is like a city broken down, without walls." In the ancient world, walls were everything. In the same way, when we neglect to control our spirits, we leave them vulnerable to attack.

Your spirit is the part of your being that responds to God and receives his power. The word *spirit* shows up hundreds and hundreds of times throughout Scripture. Here are some of the highlights:

- When you are saved, your spirit is the part of you that is most affected: "I will give you a new heart and put a new spirit in you" (Ezekiel 36:26 NIV).
- When you sin, your spirit gets off-kilter and needs recalibration, like a compass near a magnetic field: "Renew a right spirit within me" (Psalm 51:10 ESV).
- You must learn how to control your spirit and then practice doing so, especially in times of anger: "He who rules his spirit [is better] than he who takes a city" (Proverbs 16:32 ESV).
- Your spirit can have good intentions, but it can be overcome by sinful desires and needs to be fortified by prayer: "The spirit indeed is willing, but the flesh is weak" (Mark 14:38 ESV).
- A calm spirit causes you to have a quiet confidence: "A man of understanding is of a calm spirit" (Proverbs 17:27).
- We can ask God for a spirit marked by generosity just like his: "Uphold me by Your generous Spirit" (Psalm 51:12).

♦ An extraordinary spirit leads to open doors and promotion: "Daniel became distinguished above all the [others] . . . , because an excellent spirit was in him" (Daniel 6:3 ESV).

♦ God is drawn to those who have a spirit marked by humility and those who lift their eyes to him when in pain: "The Lord . . . saves such as have a contrite spirit" (Psalm 34:18).

Learning how to steer your spirit by managing your thoughts is incredibly important. If your spirit is out of control, it's difficult to put your life under God's control. And a spirit under God's control is key to advancing in this war.

So I want you to keep hold of these three things as we move forward. First, no matter how much of the day has been spent, *it's not too late to change course.* Not tomorrow but right now. Second, having a name for the version of you that you don't want to be helps you *call yourself out* when you're behaving badly. Decide on a name for your own version of *Evilevi*. Once you have a name for your alter ego, you can mark it off the guest list. Third, *new mercies* are only a prayer, a breath, a short walk, or even a sip of water away. Don't be afraid to use props if your spirit is about to be taken hostage by a bad mood. Slip your ear buds in. Throw a song on. Close your eyes for a little bit. Buy a small set of watercolors to keep with you. Figure out what your bliss is so that you can hit reset on what you believe you are stuck on inside.

Escaping your self-imposed hostage situation might not be as easy as hopping on the moving sidewalk that brought you there, but that's okay—you can take the stairs.

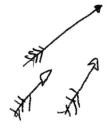

Prayer

Father, fill me afresh in this moment with a new measure of your grace and with new mercies for the day. I surrender control of my spirit and give it to you. Amen.

BREATHE, THINK, AND LIVE

× Describe your last bad mood or two. What were the circumstances surrounding it?

× If you got in it, what kept you from getting out of it?

× What's your *Evilevi*'s name? Describe what he or she is like.

× What's your typical threshold for giving up on a day? When do you call it a lost cause?

× What kinds of bad decisions usually accompany such a write-off?

× How, practically, can you approach God's throne of grace when a day has been tainted? I'm talking a quick emergency prayer you can say nine times or ninety-nine times a day to ask for grace to turn it around.

× How are your moods or internal battles more important and related to your external battles than you might have previously thought?

× What ways will you care for your spirit today? What's your emergency chill-out plan?

Day 17

HHT HHT HHT II

FLIP YOUR THOUGHTS

⚡ Rejoice always. ⚡

1 Thessalonians 5:16

I have known a lot of people in the church who sneer at the idea of positive thinking, as though it were somehow a betrayal of the gospel. It seems to be one of those things some Christians love to bash (along with global warming, secular music, and evolution). A while back I realized that, almost without fail, those who are quick to look down their noses at the power of positive thinking and view it as a carnal and unspiritual thing also happen to be pretty negative people. This much I know for sure: the more I've paid attention to the positives and negatives in my mind, the more I've liked the positive direction of my life.

Don't misunderstand me. I don't believe in positive thinking as a replacement for God but as a response to God. My goal isn't that you would see your metaphorical cup as half full; I want you to see it as constantly overflowing!

What is faith if not a filter that allows you to process your experiences through the goodness of God, choosing to reject what you see and clinging to what you trust he is doing? Faith allows you to believe your beliefs and doubt your doubts.

Yet sometimes people go too far and make positive thinking the be-all and end-all. Don't let that put you off. Just because something can be done the wrong way doesn't mean it isn't ever right.

Positive thinking isn't evil; in fact, you will see just the opposite in Scripture. It's not offensive to God; it's obedience to him. The shortest verse in the Bible makes that crystal clear: "Rejoice always" (1 Thessalonians 5:16). (Oh yes, it is the shortest. In the original Greek, "Jesus wept" is sixteen characters, and "Rejoice always" is only fourteen, making it the shortest verse. Pow.)

But don't let its size fool you; this little guy packs a punch. It is both powerful and challenging.

Rejoice always? Think about that. Not some of the time or when things are going great, but always.

Paul tells us specifically that ever-present joy is a part of God's plan for our lives: "Rejoice always, pray without ceasing, in everything give thanks; for this is the will of God in Christ Jesus for you" (1 Thessalonians 5:16–18).

With these commands ("rejoice," "pray," "give thanks"), he's not only telling us the will of God; he's giving us tools. It is impossible to do those things and be negative at the same time. When you feel like complaining, see yourself acting selfishly, or find yourself slipping into a bad mood, shoot a prayer to God that is full of joy and gratitude instead. *Setting your mind on things above you is declaring war on low-level thinking.*

If you let negativity in the door, it will want a seat at the table. And if you

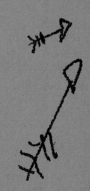

REJOICE ALWAYS.

—1 THESSALONIANS 5:16

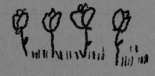

give it a seat at the table, it will want to sleep in your bed. Soon negativity becomes your default mode.

Trust me when I tell you many people struggle with this. In the Bible there's Elijah, Jonah, and Paul for a start. And there's me. My dad actually nicknamed me "Mr. Negative" when I was in high school. You are most assuredly not alone in your battle to keep your mind from drifting into negativity. But this battle isn't going anywhere. If you think, *I can't wait until I mature so this won't be an issue anymore*, you're setting yourself up for disappointment. There is truth to the expression "new levels, new devils." If anything, the battle against negativity grows more complex as you progress in your spiritual journey, because the more you do, the more the Enemy will try to stop you.

It is so important that we nail this concept down right now. Why? Because *your words and actions both begin as thoughts.* To quote a great line from the cinematic masterpiece *Kung Fu Panda 3*: "Before battle of fist must come battle of mind." Listen to me carefully: negative thoughts can't lead to a positive life. You probably never wake up and think, *I want to have a bad day* or *I want to be a bummer to be around* or *I want to suck the joy out of people I encounter.* But we all have allowed ourselves to think the kinds of thoughts that lead to a negative day.

That means you can change the way you feel by changing the way you think.

I'm not advocating for a fluffy, self-help type of positive thinking in which you naively believe that because you tell yourself everything is going to be fine, it automatically will be. Remember, this isn't a glass-half-full type of optimism; that's much too small. I am talking about a *life-to-the-full* positivity. It's true you have a God who anoints your head with oil, causes goodness and mercy to follow you all the days of your life, and prepares a table for you (Psalm 23:5–6). But let's remember that the table he is preparing for you is situated in the presence of your enemies—which presupposes you have enemies. And you do. Internally, externally, spiritually, professionally, relationally. People will oppose you if you are on the right track. We tend to ask, *What did I do wrong?* But the better question would be, *What did I do right?*

Jesus said, "Woe to you when all men speak well of you" (Luke 6:26). That goes against our obsession with pleasing people, but you can't please God and man at the same time.

Of course, people will try to take a bite out of you when you dare to do something great. For many of them it will be the only taste of greatness they will ever have! Factor opposition into your positive thinking. You can't be blindsided by what you are prepared for. Come up with contingencies and backups. If you fail to plan, you are planning to fail. Keep planning and flipping, and you'll rewrite the story you tell in your head.

In the book *Extreme Ownership: How US Navy SEALs Lead and Win*, the authors, two former Navy SEALs, tell of a phrase they have made a ritual. No matter what happens to them in the midst of all manner of madness coming their way, they choose to think in response, *Good times.* That response puts them in the proper frame of mind to stay strong and increases their effectiveness. In essence, they are taking a potentially negative situation and seeing it from a different perspective. Psychologists call this tactic *cognitive restructuring.* It allows them then to be on their toes and not on their heels as they move forward.

I dare you to try it.

Dishwasher broken? Good. Now I'll get some time to think and listen to a podcast while I wash dishes by hand.

It's raining again? Good. I love the smell of rain.

I realize this may seem fine for dishwashers and bad weather, but it doesn't feel big enough to counter the horrible hardships you have been through. I feel you. But the way to use the word *good* that will cause the wolf to rise in your heart isn't to say that the bad thing is good but to believe that goodness will be the end result.

David, a Navy SEAL of the Old Testament, focused on goodness this way when he wrote, "I would have lost heart, unless I had believed that I would see the goodness of the LORD in the land of the living" (Psalm 27:13).

The ultimate goodness of God's plans is what was on Paul's heart when he instructed the Thessalonians, "Rejoice always, pray without ceasing, in everything give thanks; for this is the will of God in Christ Jesus for you" (1 Thessalonians 5:16–18).

Did you catch that? He didn't say to be thankful *for* everything. You aren't supposed to be thankful *for* death or divorce or unemployment. Those things aren't good. You can, however, be thankful *in* those things—or in any other thing hell can throw at you—because God has a plan to produce good from what you are facing.

That's what we're ultimately getting at when we talk about your ability to reverse negative to positive. Flip your mind and make it stick. They don't call it a mindset for no reason. You have to set your mind. Give it a try. It'll work. I'm positive.

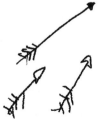

Prayer

Father, I declare war on low-level thinking and set my mind on things above. Keep my mind from negative thinking and fill my heart with gratitude. Amen.

BREATHE, THINK, AND LIVE

x Have you ever scoffed at positive thinking or tried it and found it lacking? What do you think could be missing from your previous attempts that you're willing to try as you fight this battle in your mind?

x How and when do you typically find yourself getting negative? Name a few topics of conversation or situations that typically get your back up (like the dishwasher example).

x What counterphrase could you use to flip yourself from negative to positive?

x If negativity has worn down a groove in your brain, what phrase can you think up for yourself that's going to act like a Navy SEAL's "good times" to get you in a different groove? (A simple phrase, a Bible verse, anything could work. Just make it short and memorable.)

x What's your contingency plan for when people try to bust up your positive attitude? Think strategically. *Who* is likely to do this? *What* will they do? *When* will they do it? *Where* is this likely to go down? *Why* are they not going to succeed where they normally would? *How* are you going to stick up for a positive mindset?

x Gratitude, prayer, thanksgiving. How can you make these practices a part of your daily life so you can have them at hand when negativity strikes?

Day 18

~~||||~~ ~~||||~~ ~~||||~~ |||

MIND YOUR WORDS

 The tongue has the power of life and death,
and those who love it will eat its fruit.

Proverbs 18:21 NIV

We've been talking about the power of thoughts. Now we're going to focus on what happens when your thoughts hit your mouth. Words are powerful whether you're saying them to yourself or to other people, or someone's saying them to you. You can't win the war with the version of yourself you don't want to be if you focus only on sticks and stones and think that words can never hurt you. They can *definitely* hurt you. But they can also help you—and everyone else in your life.

Words are my life. They are what I do. I have spent thousands and thousands of hours laboring over very precise wording: arranging outlines, message points, chapters, paragraphs, sentences. I mull over plays on words, end rhymes, beginning rhymes, and alliteration. My mom would (and if I am completely honest, sometimes Jennie still does) catch me silently mouthing something I just said a second time to roll it around and test its rhythmic quality.

Here's the problem: an unguarded strength is a double weakness. If you flip over any virtue, you'll find vice on the bottom. Whatever comes naturally to you can easily become a problem for you.

There's no other area that is easier (for me) to mess up, and that has caused more heartache afterward than talking. I've shot my mouth off and felt remorse so regularly that it is a great source of sadness for me. I measure how well a meeting went not by the number of good ideas I had or whether the content was covered but by whether it ends without my having said something I want to take back.

You know that feeling when you walk away from a conversation and the perfect insult comes to your mind just a minute too late? ("Well, the Jerk Store called, and they're running out of you!") The French have a term for it: *esprit de l'escalier.* It's the witty comeback you think of after you've left the situation. There is science behind why that happens: when you're in a confrontation, the limbic portion of your brain kicks into fight-or-flight mode, allocating all available resources into keeping you alive. Unfortunately, both cleverness and people skills suffer. Once the moment passes, the blood that was being diverted to your muscles and to your vision with a shot of adrenaline returns to the rational part of your brain, so you are able to think of what you couldn't in the moment.

I wish I had that feeling more often. The feeling I have more regularly is, *Why didn't I put a hand over my mouth and not say the thing I thought of?*

Tragically, words are like toothpaste; once they're out of the tube, there's no putting them back in.

The book of Proverbs says that the tongue contains the power of both life and death (18:21). It's like a tiny nuclear reactor capable of being both an energy plant that lights up a town and a bomb that can destroy a city.

All things that can do much good can also do great evil. Bricks can be used to build hospitals or be thrown through windows. Water can quench a thirst or flood a city. Likewise, words are neutral in and of themselves; it's how you use them that determines whether they are good or bad.

That is the argument James makes in one of the most powerful statements on speech ever put into words (pun intended):

> Indeed, we put bits in horses' mouths that they may obey us, and we turn their whole body. Look also at ships: although they are so large and are driven by fierce winds, they are turned by a very small rudder wherever the pilot desires. Even so the tongue is a little member and boasts great things.
>
> See how great a forest a little fire kindles! And the tongue is a fire, a world of iniquity. The tongue is so set among our members that it defiles the whole body, and sets on fire the course of nature; and it is set on fire by hell. . . . Out of the same mouth proceed blessing and cursing. My brethren, these things ought not to be so. (3:3–6, 10)

James explained that one tiny spark—a cigarette thrown out a car window or an improperly doused campfire—can lead to an inferno that burns down a whole forest. In the same way, a single sentence can alter your life: "I love you." "Will you marry me?" "It's a boy." "I want a divorce." "I forgive you." "I'm sorry."

A sentence can devastate: "We're going to have to let you go." "It's cancer." "There's nothing more we can do."

But it can just as easily cause you to celebrate: "You're being promoted!" "You have the golden ticket!" "Your long-lost aunt left you an enormous inheritance!"

Words can cost you your job. Don Imus had a successful radio career, but he was brought down by uttering a racial slur. Words can cost you your life; mouth off to the wrong person and get yourself killed.

Just as heredity controls what kind of tongue you have—whether you can roll it up or how long it is—heredity is also the reason our tongues are so destructive. We read in Romans that it's our sinful nature that makes our words so dangerous: "Through one man sin entered the world, and death through sin, and thus death spread to all men, because all sinned" (5:12).

Fortunately, whatever can be used for evil can be reclaimed and used for good. The tongue can be set on fire by hell, but it can also be set on fire by heaven.

While under control of the Holy Spirit, Peter, who had cursed Christ and denied knowing him, preached the gospel to the saving of two thousand souls on the day of pentecost. Proverbs 25:11 tells us, "A word fitly spoken is like apples of gold in settings of silver." If your speech is filled with grace (Colossians 4:6), your words will have the same impact salt (or Tabasco sauce) has on food: they will make things better! Then your words can build people up, share the gospel, pray for the sick. Your words can encourage, comfort, reassure, and make people laugh.

Proverbs 27:17 says, "As iron sharpens iron, so a friend sharpens a friend"

(NLT). Sometimes you need to speak difficult words that are necessary to help people become who they were born to be. In a sense, love will ask you to stab your friends in the front. And that's a good thing!

When the tongue is working properly, it is both a spring that refreshes and a fruit tree that nourishes. A runaway horse is dangerous, and a boating accident can end in disaster. But when the bit is firmly in place, and the rudder steers correctly, you can enjoy scenery that is both beautiful and pleasurable.

Paul instructed the Ephesians to choose their words carefully. Consider *The Message*'s translation of his teaching: "Watch the way you talk. Let nothing foul or dirty come out of your mouth. Say only what helps, each word a gift" (4:29 THE MESSAGE). What could happen if the words you used weren't foul or dirty but rather were gifts for those you were speaking to? What if they were gifts to yourself?

On average, sixteen thousand words come out of your mouth per day. We want to enlist all of them to help, not hinder, the cause we're fighting for. Today, turn your mind to your words, and knowing their power, enlist them to your cause.

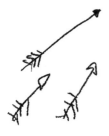

Prayer

Father, fill my speech with grace so that out of my mouth will come words of life, refreshment, encouragement, and praise. Be the Lord of lips. Amen.

BREATHE, THINK, AND LIVE

- How have you felt the impact of words? What are some words you can remember that have built you up or changed your life for the better?
- What about for the worse?
- What are some words you regret saying to others?
- List some things you say to yourself that tear you down.
- If we think of those words as "foul and dirty," which opposing words could be a gift?
- Take a day to watch the way you talk. Keep a mental tab on your conversations and interactions, no matter how brief.
  - Are there any places you want to change course with your typical words?
  - Any places you want to insert more encouragement or gifts to people?
  - Any places that, rather than tearing down or building up, might be wasted opportunities to use good words?
  - Any places where you're using nice words instead of truthful or difficult words said in love?
- Think of your tongue as a rudder. Where's it steering you now? What kind of words might steer you where you want to go in life? How, where, and with whom will you use them to change your course?

Day 19

|||| |||| |||| ||||

CHANGE THE OUTCOME

 Truly I tell you, if you have faith as small as a mustard seed, you can say to this mountain, "Move from here to there," and it will move. Nothing will be impossible for you.

Matthew 17:20 NIV

One of my favorite Bible stories illustrates the capacity your attitude and your words have to set the tone for your faith and for your future.

A centurion—an officer in the Roman army in charge of a hundred men—came to Jesus for help because his servant was seriously ill. Centurions were career soldiers, hardened men of war. It was difficult to become a centurion, but once you got the position, you had it made. He had money, power, respect. In other words, he was living the dream.

On the other hand, slaves in the Roman Empire had no rights; they weren't classified as human beings but rather as "living tools." Slaves significantly outnumbered the empire's seventy million citizens, and so maintaining the illusion of control was imperative for the masters, who knew there would be little they could do to stop a mutiny if the ants ever figured out that they didn't need to give all their food to the grasshoppers. (Sorry not sorry. I love Disney.)

When a slave was sick and unable to work, masters were under no obligation to seek out medical attention, because they could just as easily buy a replacement. Knowing that, you can immediately see there was something different about this soldier. He showed no trace of cruelty, only tenderness as he sought help on behalf of his servant. The attitude of his heart and the words he used show that he considers the young man to be like a son to him: "Lord, my servant is lying at home paralyzed, dreadfully tormented" (Matthew 8:6). In reference to Jesus, he used the word *Lord*; in Greek, the word is *kurios*, which means king. This was nothing short of a profession of faith in Jesus as his sovereign.

In response to the centurion's pleas, Jesus immediately agreed to come to the man's home to treat his servant. But the centurion protested. There was no need for Jesus to enter his home. First, it would have been inconvenient for Jesus to travel; second, if Jesus had entered the house of a Gentile, he would have been ceremonially defiled, and he would have had to go through a cleansing ritual before his daily life could continue. (Translation: he would have gotten Gentile cooties.) The centurion didn't want Jesus to be put out while doing him a favor.

Instead, the centurion trusted that Jesus' words would be enough: "Only speak a word, and my servant will be healed" (v. 8). His logic is sound. If Jesus was the Word, all he needed to do was speak the word, and the servant would be fine. The creation has no choice but to respond to the Creator.

The centurion's faith astonished Jesus: "When Jesus heard it, He marveled"

(v. 10). That's noteworthy, because Jesus was a difficult guy to impress! He continued, "I have not found such great faith, not even in Israel!" (v. 10). Though the centurion was not one of God's people, he demonstrated the behavior—a heart of faith articulated through lips confessing belief in what God can do—that God had sought from the very beginning.

Jesus had never performed a miracle in the way this man was suggesting. Until this point, he had always been physically present when he healed people; he touched them or prayed over them or rubbed mud in their eyes. What the centurion suggested was a long-distance miracle, which suggests a whole other level of faith in Jesus.

Jesus' response to the centurion included three incredible words that held great promise long before they were sung by Paul McCartney and John Lennon: "As you have believed, so *let it be* done for you" (v. 13, emphasis added).

This phrase—*let it be*—is actually where we get the word *amen* from. We usually use amen at the end of our prayers, as though to say, "May what I have prayed come to pass." But in light of the story of Jesus and the centurion, our goal should be to pray such gutsy prayers that God says amen to us.

Faith is the password that unlocks God's power. Jesus said, "If you have faith as a mustard seed, you will say to this mountain, 'Move from here to there,' and it will move; and nothing will be impossible for you" (Matthew 17:20). The Roman soldier had enough faith to ask for a long-distance miracle, and as a result, Jesus granted his request and moved the mountain. The centurion received a miracle because he had faith that made Jesus marvel. Similarly, *your goal should be to use your words in such a way that they bless the heart of God, inspire faith in those around you, and make life better for those who are hurting.*

God is saying that impossible things can be done when you speak faith in the midst of the storm, though sometimes the impossible thing is you continuing to believe in him in the middle of it all, even when what you're believing for doesn't happen. He's not saying you're going to get every single thing you want if you just speak to it in an attitude of faith. Always, Jesus' attitude is "Thy will be done, not mine." We're not in some warped reality distortion field where we say, "My Honda Accord is now a Ferrari." *Poof!* Well, what do you know? The mountain got moved, right?

That's not what we're talking about here. We're not believing that our faith is some sort of bottle that we rub with good words, causing a genie to pop out and grant us our three wishes. That's not what words spoken in an attitude of faith do.

Jesus Christ didn't come to give us a blank check for any dream. But when hard days come, the way we speak in the midst of our crisis, in the midst of our difficulty, can cause something to happen that feels impossible. A mountain of discouragement can move. A mountain of ingrained negativity can move. A mountain of hopelessness can move. It happens when we do things like speaking words of faith in the midst of a chemotherapy treatment. Suddenly we have more to give and joy where there shouldn't be any.

The impossible happens because of how you speak about it. You determine to speak words of blessing. Of positivity. Of faith in God. Of encouragement to everyone you encounter. It's all about how you speak to your difficulty. You can't be a victim and a victor at the same time. And in these cases, how you speak can change the future. It can alter the course of history.

Believe that God is going to bring good out of the worst times, and speak it. The devil's not getting the last word.

Maybe you struggle with being bitter because life has been hard, other people have had it easier, and you feel you would have more rosy things to say if rosier things happened to you. But you don't have to do a lot when it comes to words.

Dr. Seuss knew this. He tried to use as few different words as he could when writing. He imposed his own constraints, which liberated him to write better books because he had fewer options. He wrote *The Cat in the Hat* with 236 different words, so his editor bet him he couldn't write a book using only 50 different words. He won the bet when he wrote *Green Eggs and Ham*, one of the best-selling books of all time.

This illustration is even cooler because *Green Eggs and Ham* is about a guy who is anti-everything. He doesn't like anything, and everything is soured by his bad attitude. Only when he tries the thing he thinks he hates does he change his mindset and attitude. When that one thing clicked into place, his whole world changed from negative to positive.

Perhaps you have huge untapped potential but a rebellious spirit that manifests itself in words that are negative and mean, sarcastic and harsh, and that overrules everything. Could it be that words of humility and submission flowing from a heart that accepts God's sovereignty and his goodness could lead to a whole new world of God's using you? He could use you to do great things, no matter where you go or what you do. Whether you are in a boat. With a goat. Wearing socks. Or with a fox!

It's crazy to think about how much of a difference your attitude can make. Did you know fans have the ability to change the outcome of a sporting event? They can sit there with their arms crossed or open their mouths and cheer. A researcher from Harvard University discovered that crowd noise has a verifiable impact on

EXPECTANCY
AND
EXCITEMENT
CHANGE
EVERYTHING.

the game; for every ten thousand fans present, a home team gains an additional 0.1 goal advantage. One person cheering is not so loud, but a whole arena? That's a whole different matter. *Expectancy and excitement change everything.*

When your words are full of faith, impossible things can be accomplished. Mountains can move. This doesn't mean there won't be times when you speak words of faith with an attitude of hope and see nothing happen. In those moments, the most important thing is to remember that some of God's most important miracles can't be seen with the naked eye. He knows what you need to know. Sometimes the mountain that needs moving is inside you.

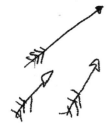

Prayer

Thank you, Father, that nothing is impossible for you! Give me a long-distance, far-reaching, abundant faith that will move mountains and stir up miracles. I believe. Amen.

 BREATHE, THINK, AND LIVE

- x Why do you think the centurion's words to Jesus were so impressive?
- x Do you believe that with a word from Jesus, your situations can change? Why or why not?
- x What percentage of the words you speak (inside or outside of church)

pertain to faith in God and his goodness? How can you speak more in your daily life (with your mouth, not just your mind) in ways that bless God?

x What about words of humility and submission? Where could some of your words that give off meanness or sarcasm make a critical swap to words that acknowledge that God is sovereign?

x What about words of hopelessness or defeat? Where could you exchange them for words of expectancy and excitement?

— Sit down with a Bible and something to take notes with. We're going to find some words to help you move mountains in you. Do you believe God is for you? If so, why? Write down words to express that here and state them out loud. Find scripture to back that up, and say, "Amen. Let it be."

— Do you believe God is working even the crappy situations in your life for good? Put it in words, speak them, add a scripture to seal them, and say, "Amen. Let it be."

— Do you believe that God is good? Put it in your words, speak them, find scriptures, and say, "Amen. Let it be."

— Do you believe God empowers you to take back your life from the things that hold you down? You know the drill. Use your words and find backup in the Word of God. Make it a habit and a commitment to speak words of life in this battle you're fighting.

Day 20

HHT HHT HHT HHT

TAKE BACK THE CONTROLS

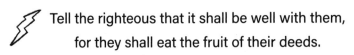 Tell the righteous that it shall be well with them,
for they shall eat the fruit of their deeds.

Isaiah 3:10 ESV

Little by little we make our choices, and then our choices make us. The philosopher Will Durant observed, "We are what we repeatedly do." We've talked about thoughts and words and attitudes. Today I am going to talk about why habits and decisions you repeat are a really big deal.

The robots are taking over. Alexa. Siri. Automatic lane assist. It's a brave new world overflowing with automation. More and more things happen on their own without the need for human involvement. I don't bring this up to make you fear the automation happening all around you but to bring to your attention the automation happening inside you. It's not just cars and homes and washing machines and websites that have become automated. Your behavior has as well. Your thoughts, your words, how you respond to your moods, what feelings you act on, how you talk to your husband or wife, the way you treat those in authority, and how you speak to yourself are all like water dripping on a rock that eventually wears down a groove. Given enough time, it can become the Grand Canyon.

Board-formed concrete is made by pouring concrete into wooden forms, where it will dry and set up. Your habits are like one of those forms, and time is the concrete we pour into it. That means it is absolutely code-blue critical that you declare war, and do it now. You'll have time to think about the implications later. You haven't got a moment to lose. You can't afford to put off change until tomorrow; it's now or never. *Your habits are hardening as we speak.*

It's just how your brain operates. It seeks to conserve its limited resources in order to have processing power available for what you need. Anything you do repeatedly it seeks to chunk together into a routine. According to research from Duke University, about 45 percent of our actions each day are habits. That means that close to half of your life you're not actually thinking carefully about what you are doing but are running through an automated ritual baked into your being.

That can be a good thing or a bad thing, depending on what your habits are. Buckling up when you get into your car? Great. Clamming up when you get your feelings hurt? Not so great.

It's critical to examine what your habits are. Bad habits put you at a decided disadvantage, regardless of what you do the rest of the time. You might have the noblest intentions to honor God or be a person of character, but bad relational, financial, or physical habits can hold you back. If it's true that 45 percent of your life is on autopilot, you are already hamstrung in your attempts to live the life you want, because you are working with only 55 percent of your energy, time, and attention. It's an enormous handicap to overcome.

On the other hand, if you pour healthy habits into the concrete, the right choices become automatic. You don't have to try nearly as hard if you can get your habits to work for you. Your habits either put the wind in your face or at your back. The right ones need to stay, and the wrong ones need to go.

One particularly bad habit that threatens our ability to achieve greatness is our addiction to our screens. Americans spend up to five hours a day on our phones. Almost a third of the time we're awake, we're hunched over glowing screens. That's more time given to any other activity in our lives besides sleeping. A hundred fifty hours a month checking emails, sending texts, playing the newest game, shopping online, putting dog ears and noses on our faces, reading blogs, selecting GIFs and emojis, and catching up on Twitter. Over the course of a lifetime, that adds up to about *fourteen years*.

And get this. When you haven't touched your device in a while, your brain releases a stress hormone called cortisol in a plot to trigger another hit of dopamine, and you feel afraid you might be missing out on something. Justin Rosenstein, the man who created the Facebook like button, now describes likes as "bright dings of pseudo-pleasure."

It's unfortunate but true: the conditioned response of compulsively refreshing our email in-boxes or messages or social accounts doesn't satisfy you. It only deepens your dependence and leaves you like an alcoholic craving another drink.

The robots are taking over, all right. Only we are the robots, jumping every time the ping sounds and drooling every time the bell rings. How are you ever going to do all the great things God has called you to do if you give away that much control of yourself? What else could you do with those fourteen years?

I recently read David McCullough's *The American Spirit: Who We Are and What We Stand For*, and his description of Thomas Jefferson stopped me dead in my tracks: "He read seven languages. He was a lawyer, surveyor, ardent meteorologist, botanist, agronomist, archaeologist, paleontologist, Indian ethnologist, classicist, and brilliant architect. Music, he said, was the passion of his soul; mathematics, the passion of his mind."

Are you kidding me? I read that paragraph out loud to Jennie and remarked, "This is why he was able to write the Declaration of Independence." Which, by the way, he wrote at age thirty-three.

If you put down your phone for a few minutes, picked up books a little more, and took up a hobby like paleontology or botany or, heck, why not both and six more, perhaps you, too, would be capable of creating something that could change the world.

The world doesn't need another Declaration of Independence, but it does desperately need to see the greatness Jesus has given you—greatness that is bursting to come out. But first you have to win the war with yourself before it can ever see the light of day.

The habits you allow in your life today are going to determine who you become tomorrow. Future you is an exaggerated version of current you. *Time doesn't change anything; it merely deepens and reveals who we are.* If you are kind today, you will be kinder tomorrow. If you are cruel today, that, too, will deepen. Smile lines or frowning wrinkles are forming on your face at this very moment. Generous old people are people who, when they were young, lived lives of generosity, and cranky old people grew out of young people who never learned to get out of their own way.

At a commencement speech, David McCullough spoke to a generation that is addicted to the internet and has lost sight of simple pleasures: "Sometime, somewhere along the line, memorize a poem. Sometime, somewhere along the line, go out in a field and paint a picture, for your own pleasure. Sometime, somewhere along the line, plant a tree, buy your father a good bottle of New York state wine, write your mother a letter."

Whatever new habits you decide on, make sure to write them down. Those who commit their goals to paper are 42 percent more likely to accomplish them and earn nine times as much over their lifetimes as people who don't.

You'll need those new habits to break the bad ones. It will feel really uncomfortable to jettison behavior that has been with you for a long time. It may feel awkward to try something new. Your desire for comfort will beg you to go back to how it used to be. But you mustn't relent from what you wrote down when you chose to declare war. It might not feel good in the moment, but that's where the fight comes in. Decide you'll do it and start setting good habits that will solidify over time into lifelong strengths.

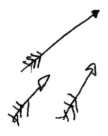

Prayer

Father, reveal to me my blind spots, the choices I've been making that have now made me. Teach me and strengthen me to form war-winning habits. Amen.

BREATHE, THINK, AND LIVE

x Think about your autopilot habits and the little decisions you make over and over again. Where are you on autopilot to a place you don't really love?

    — Relationally?

    — Financially?

    — Physically?

x What are your screen habits like? Include phone, computer, TV, tablet—anything glowy. Experiment with time tracking (there are apps for this) and give yourself a reality check. How could you cut down?

x What simple pleasures do you want to make into habits just because they're nice? How can those replace screen time?

x Think of the things you're peripherally interested in. What would you get into in life if you had an extra, say, *fourteen years* to spend on it?

x Think of the idea that time only deepens habits. What are you doing now that you don't want to be part of future you?

x What are you not doing that you *do* want to be part of future you?

x Take a moment and make five to ten habit goals. Commit them to paper and post them somewhere you can see them. How can you let these large goals start influencing your small autopilot decisions?

Day 21

COMPOUND INTEREST

 With your help I can advance against a troop;
with my God I can scale a wall.

Psalm 18:29 NIV

There is no such thing as a small decision.

Every time you make a decision, it's like a domino falling over. And everyone knows that one domino takes down the next. Physicist Hans van Leeuwen discovered that every time a domino falls, it generates a force sufficient to knock down a domino twice as big as itself. That means that in decisions, as in dominoes, we have a phenomenally powerful force on our hands. One choice affects another, and the effects of those choices accumulate and magnify over time. This is called exponential growth.

Understanding the mind-boggling phenomenon of exponential growth has the capacity to change every aspect of your life. It's the difference between

17 percent interest on $97,700 in credit card debt and 17 percent interest on that same amount tucked away in a 401(k) ($16,609 in black ink or in red ink). It's the gap between eating a hundred fewer calories and a hundred more calories than you burn each day for a year (a staggering twenty-pound difference, which is pretty wild considering a hundred calories isn't even half a Snickers bar). And that is just in a single year; carried out over a longer period, the results diverge even more.

In the time it takes for a single decade to come and go, you could have racked up a mountain of credit card debt, packed on thirty extra pounds, or smoked 36,500 cigarettes. On the flip side, you could have also used the time to become fluent in a new language, gotten a degree, and set yourself up to be financially stable and generous. Ten years is long enough to do a lot for good or for evil. Can we agree? C. S. Lewis elaborated on this idea in his classic *Mere Christianity*: "Good and evil both increase at compound interest. That is why the little decisions you and I make every day are of such infinite importance."

It is critical you take seriously the battles you are facing. It might feel like a small thing that you get in fights with your parents or your sister and frequently lose your temper. But if you can't keep your temper in check, and down the road you fly off the handle with your boss or your spouse, you might all of a sudden be out of a job or in the middle of a messy divorce. The stakes get higher; the stimuli do not. A lack of self-control now sets the stage for a future in which your emotions get the best of you. It won't be easier to win the war within when you grow up on the outside if you never did on the inside.

It's the small things—attitudes, actions, words—that matter.

Things pile up. If you're numbing your feelings with a quick hit on Amazon Prime, the Amazon boxes will pile up in your garage, but the real problem will still be there, deep down, and it will only get worse, and not better, with time. You need to learn to feel your feelings. Lean into them. Diagnose them. And then do what is needed to move through them. Distracting yourself when you're not feeling good will become a pattern you get entrenched in, and it will only ever lead to a heightened discontent.

But if you try to understand what is driving it, you can look to the Lord to fill the hole instead of the shiny trinkets and baubles of this world. You will discover that the ache you were going to silence with something on Disney+ or something made from cashmere was actually the voice of Jesus calling you to himself. It may not feel like it, but *it's a gift to be unsettled and unsatisfied because it is in those moments we can potentially find what we truly need in God himself.* The silencing of that discomfort by fast food or fast delivery from e-commerce brings the opposite—more punishment than reward.

If you are going through the motions in a way that doesn't serve you, in a way that's numbing or distracting, don't despair. Going through the motions is only bad if you're going through the wrong motions. You can pick other motions. Choosing to be vulnerable and opening up when you feel like shutting down, starting with God when you feel like rushing into the business of the day, listening when you feel like speaking, thinking when you feel like acting—these are habits that can get locked into your muscle memory too. You can get compound interest on good and evil.

An old proverb says the best time to plant a tree is twenty years ago, but the second-best time is right now. It would have been great if circumstances had been different and you didn't form bad habits to cope with them. But we can't camp there. You can't go back and change the past, but what you can do is plant a new tree of good behavior right now. Twenty years from now you will be glad you did.

THE RIGHT TIME TO DO THE RIGHT THING IS RIGHT NOW.

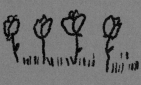

So repeat after me: the right time to do the right thing is right now. Every second you stall is time that exponential growth could be working its slow magic. If you choose to delay until tomorrow what you should be doing today, you forfeit the opportunity to power through the necessary humble beginnings for another precious twenty-four hours. There is not a moment to lose. You get into and out of things the same way: one step at a time.

Of course, the hardest part is taking that very first step. Disrupting inertia. Getting that rocket off the ground. But once you put a new habit into motion, you'll feel the wind at your back. I'm not minimizing how hard inertia is to overcome; I'm just reassuring you that, as Teddy Roosevelt discovered, there is a prize waiting for you on the other side of the barbed wire—the wolf will rise.

Bernard Roth describes this as flipping an internal switch:

Whenever anyone makes an important change, it's because a switch has flipped. Someone who has struggled her whole life with her weight finally decides to get fit. Someone who has put up with an abusive boss for years finally has enough and quits. Someone who has harbored a secret crush finally takes the plunge and asks her beloved out for coffee. A shift has happened that has made action favorable to inaction.

When you have chosen enough times to zig when you normally would have zagged, zigging will become your new normal. Objects in motion tend to stay in motion. As the brilliant researcher Charles Duhigg pointed out, habits we already have locked into place can't be deleted, but they can be overwritten. Once created, a file will always be there, but what happens when it gets triggered can be modified. He explains a habit is essentially a loop comprised of a cue, a routine, and a reward. In *The Power of Habit*, he claimed, "If you can break a habit into its components, you can fiddle with the gears.... Almost any behavior can be transformed if the cue and reward stay the same."

When you switch out the routine, the loop, on your bad habits, you can change your life, transforming what is harming you into a weapon that can help you destroy your alter ego and move you closer to becoming who you want to be.

The first few times—and maybe even the first thousand times—you respond to an old cue in a new way won't be easy. Full disclosure: it might feel unbearable. But do it long enough and you will be only a little uncomfortable. Eventually you'll feel unstoppable. When you commit yourself to the process, you'll feel like David when he exclaimed, "With your help I can advance against a troop; with my God I can scale a wall" (Psalm 18:29 NIV).

You can change your habits, your thoughts, your words, your attitudes, your deeds. You can advance and win this war one small step at a time.

The journey of a million miles has to start somewhere, and that somewhere is where you plant your shoe on the ground for the first time and believe that Providence will have your back.

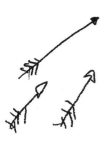

Prayer

Father, bring me to a place of dissatisfaction in the mundane. Shake me out of my settled routine so I can experience the refreshment that comes from walking with, and relying on, you. I am willing to give up what I want so I can get what I need. Amen.

BREATHE, THINK, AND LIVE

x Be honest and write down some of your bad habits. Places you don't have self-control. Places you feel numb or run to when you don't want to feel your feelings. Write down as many as you can think of here.

x Why were your bad habits created? Were they emulating a bad example? A response to pain? Maybe a feeling of being unsettled? Where did they come from?

x Some bad habits are just ineffective routes to something you really need (to relax, to celebrate, to feel soothed, etc.). What are the real goals of some of your bad habits?

x What other better habits could get you to that final goal?

x Think about the power of compound interest. Is there a habit in your life (good or bad) that you're seeing the fruit of compound interest in right now? How do you see that going in the future?

x What do you wish had been different about your habits? Why?

x Why is now the best time to start changing them?

x For your top three bad habits, identify a first step toward changing the motions you go through. It can be the tiniest baby step. What will push you out of inertia? Where will you zig where you used to zag?

WEEK 4

RUN TOWARD THE ROAR

Day 22

THE NEAREST LION

> Though a host encamp against me,
> My heart will not fear;
> Though war arise against me,
> In spite of this I shall be confident.

Psalm 27:3 NASB

I am fascinated by the way lions hunt. I've read that it's the lionesses that actually do the "lion's share" of the work. The males are obviously incredibly intimidating, with their manes and their ferocious roars, but it's the chicks you really have to watch out for.

The fact that lionesses do not have a big, recognizable mane actually helps them sneak up on whatever they are hunting. They lie in wait, hidden in the tall grass, motionless like statues. I listened to a sermon by Pastor Brian Houston of Hillsong LA in which he said that the males do play an important, albeit small role. While the females stalk their prey from behind, the king of the jungle will come from the front and let loose one of those roars that gives him his spot at the top of the food chain. This sound is so powerful it can be heard for up to five miles away. Hearing that terrifying noise causes the gazelle or antelope to run as far as they can away from whatever made that sound.

What they don't know is that as scary as it sounded, the one who did the roaring is more bark than bite. So away they go, directly into the path of the real threat: the waiting lioness. In other words, the prey's instincts are wrong. Going with their gut causes them to make the last mistake of their short little lives. It's counterintuitive, but the right choice would be to override their emotions and run toward the roar.

It's shocking how often that is true. When you run from things that scare you, you move toward danger, not away from it. If you fail to face your fears, they will always be right there behind you. You must suppress the little voice inside that's telling you to get out of Dodge. It is not your friend. When you feel that panicky fight-or-flight sensation, and you want to run away, do the opposite. Run toward the roar. You have come into the kingdom for just "such a time as this" (Esther 4:14 NASB).

Jennie and I made this decision as we chose how we were going to respond to the terrible nightmare of having our daughter taken from us. Everyone grieves differently. It's a process. But we decided that we would go through it running toward the roar. It was excruciating to go through her things. Maybe it would kill us, we thought, but if we could get through it, we wouldn't have to live in fear of closed boxes and pictures and videos. I didn't want anything sneaking up on me. No shrines, no booby traps. We faced it all, and then pushed on into the future.

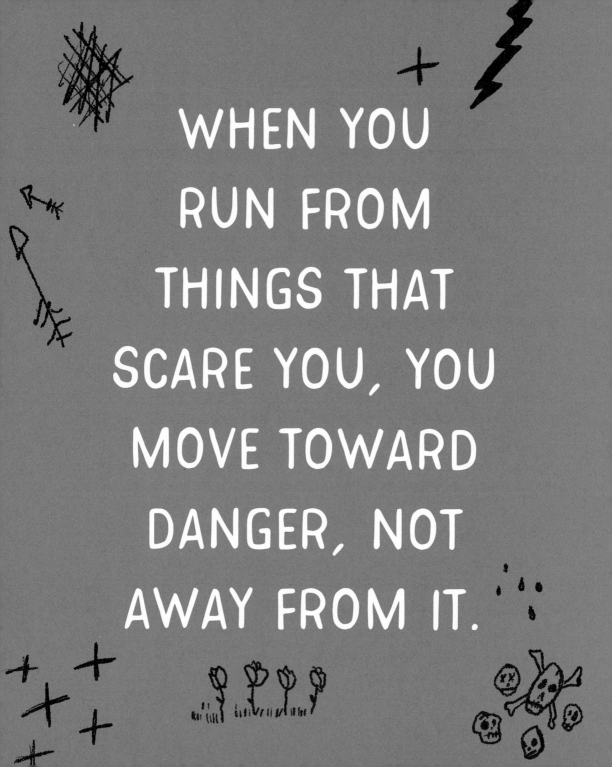

One of the most difficult days was when the hospital gave us a box with the things Lenya had been wearing in the emergency room. I didn't want to open it. We felt like running in the opposite direction. But eventually Jennie and I braced ourselves and faced it. The box contained her little socks, leggings, and the top that had been cut off her with medical scissors. All the emergency room personnel had written notes to us on a card they included in the package. At the bottom was an ink handprint and footprint an ER nurse had thoughtfully captured from Lenya's hands and feet as a keepsake.

Jennie and I wept on the floor as we pulled these items out one by one. It felt as if fire were burning underneath my skin, and my brain grew hot. The socks, more than anything, destroyed me. It was more than I could bear. We cried together and called on the Lord and prayed for the people who worked in the ER. And then we got up.

I pray you never have to have your heart pierced with a sword like that, but like it or not, in ways small and large, *we are all going to have to confront our fears or abandon our destinies.* The only path to the lives you are meant to reach is to launch out into the deep and sail through things that are scary. Smooth seas never made a skilled sailor. God calls us to go to places that frighten us so that we will fully trust him. The only way for you to do the kinds of things he desires is to run toward the roar again and again and again.

What in your life are you being called to right now? Perhaps it's a song you are meant to write or a church you are meant to plant. Maybe it's pulling your children out of school to educate them at home or allowing your son to go to a public school so he can share his faith and be salt and light. Are you vacillating between the safety of a job you hate and the terrifying prospect of starting your own business? Maybe you are supposed to go back to school or, on the other hand, it might be that you should opt out of college in order to pursue a different kind of education.

I can't tell you what God's will for your life is. There is no magic map. All I can tell you is that you must not let fear play a part in your decision-making. You can't ignore fear, but you don't have to let it control you. True bravery isn't feeling no fear. It's being afraid and moving forward anyway.

I know this for sure: turning your back on the roar will feel good in the moment. You will feel a euphoric giddiness once you have put some distance between yourself and the lunacy you were considering. *Cooler heads prevailed,* you will think as you wipe the dust off your hands and prepare to return to business as usual. But hiding in the thicket, far from the sound of the wild calling you are meant to pursue, is a far more sinister opponent you didn't even know was there: death. The death of the dreams God planted deep down inside you. The death of the life you were born to live. Like a slow leak in your tire that saps your ability to drive your car, you will have robbed yourself of the opportunity to stare down something that scared you. Live this way long enough, and the muscles of your faith will eventually atrophy. To quote the immortal William Wallace from the movie *Braveheart,* "Aye, fight and you may die. Run, and you'll live ... at least a while. And dying in your beds, many years from now, would you be willin' to trade *all* the days, from this day to that, for one chance, just one chance, to come back here and tell our enemies that they may take our lives, but they'll never take ... *our freedom!*"

Yes, running toward the roar can be excruciating, and there are no guarantees. It's also possible to misjudge the direction of the roar you are trying to run toward. It could be a dead end. When you live a life of faith, there are going to be questions that have no answers, because for there to be faith, there has to be mystery. That's just life in the deep end. It would be nice if we could have the safety of the shore and the potential of the open ocean at the same time, but that's not how it works. Nothing ventured, nothing gained. If you want to catch fish, you have to launch out where the fish live. It's the only way to take back a life worth living.

Prayer

Father, I declare today that my heart will not fear, and even in the face of it, I will rise up in confidence. Turning back feels easier, but I'm believing that charging forward in your strength will lead me to my destiny. Amen.

BREATHE, THINK, AND LIVE

x In what circumstances do you feel that panicky fight-or-flight sensation when you want to run away? For example:

— When certain topics of conversation come up

— When you're asked to perform a certain kind of task

— In some of the reflections about waging war on your thoughts, words, or habits

– When you think of a past event

– When you consider something you want to do in the future

x Is there anything in life that acts like a booby trap for you, sending you down a tunnel of fear?

x Do any of these have to do with a calling you feel on your life?

x In your past, can you identify any decisions you made based on fear? If so, did it feel good in the moment? What could you have missed? (This is not to bum you out but to help you recognize a key battleground so you can run toward the roar next time.)

x What are some decisions you've made to move toward a fear? How did they work out? Did you find them rewarding ultimately?

x From your thoughts above, identify some small roars (things that give you a tinge of nervousness/fear), some medium roars (things that give you a pit in your stomach), and some deafening roars (things that make you want to run like your hair is on fire). To strengthen your faith muscle, start by facing down one of your small roars. Do these one at a time. It could be one every day or every couple of days. Seriously, get out your calendar. Then as you find yourself getting bolder, amp up the challenge.

Day 23

IIII IIII IIII IIII
III

LET IT GO

 I consider that the sufferings of this present time are not
worth comparing with the glory that is to be revealed to us.

Romans 8:18 RSV

Often what keeps us in the shallows of life is our fear of failure. We want to launch out bravely, but we think we'll blow it and come back to shore hanging our heads. Know this: not only is failure not a bad thing, but it is a necessary thing. The only way to get to victory is to be willing to make mistakes on the way there. True overnight successes are rare. Far more often, you must keep showing up, day in and day out, until the hard, unglamorous work adds up and pays off. It's easy to misunderstand what you are seeing when you look at people taking a victory lap or receiving attention or a promotion. Their celebration is only the tip of the iceberg. Invisible to your eye is what's underwater—that is, the hell they went through on the road to success.

It took Bruno Mars an entire year to collaborate on "Uptown Funk," and it was in the trash can ten times during that time—but he kept on going. And then it became a massive global hit. In his words, it's "the biggest song I've ever been a part of." His whole life is really the testimony of what happens when you respond to adversity with grit.

He grew up poor. At one point in his journey his family was homeless and resorted to sleeping in a car. Then they moved into a one-bedroom house with no electricity or bathroom. But that didn't stop him from pouring himself into his music. When he moved from his native Hawaii to Los Angeles, he scored a deal with Motown Records but was subsequently dropped. Unfazed, he continued to plug away. He was the quintessential starving artist.

This is a different picture of what we often think of as someone making it big.

We tend to think of successful people as having a Midas touch, where everything they handle turns to gold. But listen to how Bruno described his process: "I was built for this . . . It's dedicating yourself to your craft. Spending thousands of hours in a studio learning how to write a song, learning how to play different chords, training yourself to sing. You know, to get better and better."

60 Minutes's Lara Logan asked him, does he consider himself to have "made it"?

No!

He played the Super Bowl and won two Grammys, but he doesn't consider himself to have arrived.

The point is that to envy someone's success is to completely misunderstand the nature of it. To covet the limelight and the accolades is to focus on the wrong thing. Yes, there are those who are given every advantage and people who are raised with silver spoons in their mouths, but far more often the recipe for success is simple and unpleasant. You persevere through difficulty, bad ideas, bad days, and bitterness again and again and again until something clicks. It's not sexy, but it's true.

What you are willing to do in secret is so often responsible for what happens in public. It would be nice to crank out a hit on your first attempt, but those unlucky enough to do so often end up unable to replicate their accidental success. Far better to be okay with creating some duds and, as the plucky Dory says in *Finding Nemo*, "Just keep swimming."

Perhaps, for you, running toward the roar isn't about something you're supposed to do but rather something difficult you have to go through: painful chemotherapy treatments, a divorce, a move across the country that will dislocate you from friendships that mean the world to you. Sometimes there is no other alternative but to face it.

People often tell me, "I don't know how you've managed to survive. I don't think I could do it if I were you." When I hear that kind of thing, the response in my head is often, *I don't think I can make it through this, either! But what choice have I had? No one gave me an option. I didn't sign up for this.*

When you have no alternative but to endure something you are afraid of, you can still exhibit bravery. It has everything to do with your attitude and outlook. Christmas is going to arrive each year, whether I like it or not. Santa Claus is, in fact, going to come to town, and there's nothing I can do to stop it. My choice is whether I will merely hunker down and try to survive the holidays and the painful associations that come with them or harness my pain and, in the midst of the turmoil, try to shine the light and turn off the dark for as many people as possible—and myself in the process. I'd rather run toward Christmas and Lenya's memory than hide from it.

Remember this: *God isn't scared of what you're scared of.* But you don't have to pretend like you're not frightened. Naming your fear is part of getting through it. It's also important to remember that Immanuel means "God with us." Jesus is with you. You are never alone.

Here's a little manifesto I wrote regarding our Christmastime fears. I encourage you to borrow the idea next time you are scared.

> We will celebrate the birth of the One who came to destroy death and bring light and immortality to light through the gospel. We will sing until our voices won't let us. We will preach and celebrate seeing people come to know Jesus, just as we did days after Lenya died in my arms. We will party if we can muster the courage, cry when we miss her, and collapse if we have to. Even though he slays us, we will bless his name. We always have a choice, and we choose to rejoice.

God has been with me through the flashbacks, the sleepless nights, the tears, and the lack of tears. He has been with me when I feel so condemned for my mistakes as Lenya's dad that I want to hurt myself. There are judgment calls I made in the moment that I obsess over but can't do anything about. Looking back, I feel like such a failure. I have found myself paralyzed by regret and wanting to become a crazy old recluse, replaying my life's blooper reel and muttering,

"Laces out, Marino!" But each time Jesus has been with me and given me the strength to face my fears.

He will do the same for you.

Some superwise person once observed that most people die at twenty-five and aren't buried until they're seventy-five. Don't let that happen to you. Don't let your soul stop growing because you're too afraid to move forward. Your greatest days are still to come. I dare you to believe the day will come when what you are most scared of right now will be included in your highlight reel as a triumphant victory. The only way to truly live is to run toward the roar.

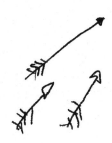

Prayer

Father, I choose to believe that the glory that is coming will not compare to the suffering of this season. Rid me of the feelings of fear, failure, and regret so I can move forward with confidence in this promise. Amen.

BREATHE, THINK, AND LIVE

× For the fears you've identified, are any of them related to a fear of failure? What's the worst that could happen if you try and fail? What's the best that could happen?

x Choose a particular fear you've named and compose a manifesto. What will you do in the face of that fear?

_____

_____

_____

_____

_____

_____

x How might what you're going through right now, the hard things, the battles, be part of the iceberg under your success?

x How could the things you're currently hiding from or pushing under the rug in life be the very things that could be your proving ground in this war?

x How does it change things to know that God isn't scared of what you're scared of? How do you plan to turn to him as these fears arise?

Day 24

TERROR BY NIGHT

 You shall not be afraid of the terror by night.

Psalm 91:5

Scary thoughts and bad dreams have been a problem for me all my days. Night terrors, sleepwalking, confusion, darkness . . . I'm more than familiar. But as someone who has struggled with fear my whole life, I'm going to share with you something wonderfully freeing. Here's what David has to say in the rest of today's scripture:

> He who dwells in the secret place of the Most High
> Shall abide under the shadow of the Almighty.
> I will say of the LORD, "He is my refuge and my fortress;
> My God, in Him I will trust." . . .

You shall not be afraid of the terror by night,

Nor of the arrow that flies by day,

Nor of the pestilence that walks in darkness,

Nor of the destruction that lays waste at noonday.

A thousand may fall at your side,

And ten thousand at your right hand;

But it shall not come near you. . . .

Because you have made the LORD, who is my refuge,

Even the Most High, your dwelling place. (Psalm 91:1–2, 5–7, 9)

Did you catch that? God promises that if you make him your God, you don't have to be afraid of terror by night! The "terror by night" David talks about has been a great source of anxiety and has stolen so much peace from so many of us. But if I "abide under the shadow of the Almighty"—put nothing above God in my heart—then the terror by night cannot touch me.

But don't miss this, because it is a huge distinction: *just because you don't have to fear evil doesn't mean you'll never feel afraid.*

Protection isn't the same as exemption. Following Jesus doesn't put you in a luxury box seat in life. You are going to be in the thick of it, your face marred by dust and sweat and grime as you charge headlong into action, knowing God both goes before you and stands as your rear guard. Your nostrils will be filled with smoke and the coppery smell of blood as your unseen enemies get close enough to make you feel like you're in danger. The spiritual support God

FOLLOWING JESUS DOESN'T PUT YOU IN A LUXURY BOX SEAT IN LIFE.

provides is not a hermetically sealed bubble suit; it is a living and active phalanx of protection in a high-stakes combat situation. Following God means being on the front lines of a battle and knowing he's got your back.

We can see how this played out in Jesus' life. God brought him safely through the battles he faced—including death—but that didn't mean he was never attacked. In fact, his public ministry was bookended by two extreme battles with fear: the temptation in the wilderness and his suffering in the Garden of Gethsemane.

Mark wrote of Jesus' temptation (1:12–13), describing how over a period that amounts to nearly six weeks, Satan tempted Jesus constantly, waging a nonstop spiritual battle that continued around the clock. During these days of terror in the wilderness, awful thoughts went through Jesus' head: *You should worship Satan. You should throw yourself off this building. You should give up on dying on the cross. And* (this is how I know the incarnation was legit and Jesus was totally human) *you should ditch your diet and eat carbs!*

These kinds of thoughts steal peace and cause terror. They might even feel familiar to you. But had Jesus given in to them, it would have taken him off the track God intended for his life.

Near the end of his ministry, Jesus experienced deep despair in the Garden of Gethsemane: "He plunged into a sinkhole of dreadful agony" (Mark 14:33 THE MESSAGE). He was so crushed by his thoughts, by this whole final scene, that capillaries under his skin began to burst, and blood began to go into his sweat glands.

What did Jesus do in those situations when he needed to cross the barbed wire and rise from his knees?

I. HE SET A SENTRY

Every time the devil attacked Jesus in the desert, he responded by quoting God's Word. He confronted lies with truth, saying, "It is written . . ." "It is written . . ." "It is written . . ." These words were his weapons of protection. It is significant that the record of this interaction doesn't say he pulled out Scripture and looked up a verse. He had these words committed to memory.

Setting God's Word before you like a sentry guarding a citadel allows you to defend your borders proactively. Filling your heart with truth causes it to be inhospitable to terror. When it is soaked in praise and steeped in Scripture, the Enemy cannot gain traction.

If you leave food out, it will attract bugs. What are you leaving out that attracts worry and fear? If you're allowing negative thoughts, if you're allowing grumbling, if you're cynical, if you're gossipy, if you have a glass-is-half-empty mentality, if you're selfish, if you're proud. All of these things are the works of the flesh. Terror grabs ahold of this stuff, and it will never be satisfied.

Ditch the things terror thrives on. Starve your fear and feed your faith. Scripture shores up the perimeter and gives the Enemy nothing to eat.

2. HE TOLD GOD ABOUT IT

When Jesus was in the grips of the terror by night, he told God what he was afraid of. He got on his knees and told his Father, *I'm afraid of the mission you gave me. I know you want me to do it, but I'm terrified of it. Could you find some other way?*

He named his fear, and as he verbalized it, he distanced himself from it. The Enemy wants to isolate you in a loop of loneliness, going around and around and around in your mind. He hopes you will keep your fear a secret so he can smother you and suffocate you and steal your peace in silence. The moment you take that fear to God, everything changes. *Bringing it to him shines light on it.* You've forced the fear to the feet of the Father, where it has no choice but to look up at him in terror.

Will what you are afraid of go away? Sometimes it will. Maybe you'll pray and *boom*! Instant miracle. In Jesus' case, God didn't change his plan, but Jesus was able to face the cross with God's help. That's the way to pray. Tell God your fear, but use a tone that says, "Not my will, but yours be done" (Luke 22:42 NIV).

3. HE CALLED FOR BACKUP

Jesus woke up his friends. He walked the ten paces to where the disciples were sleeping and said, in effect, "Hey, Peter! James! John! I'm scared right now and really alone. I have been praying, but could you maybe say a little prayer for me too?" (Matthew 26:36–41, author's paraphrase).

Do you know how much strength comes from getting people to pray for you? As kids, we had the sense to wake our parents up when we had nightmares. But somewhere along the journey, we stopped telling others we were afraid. If the Son of God knew to wake up a couple of buddies and ask them to pray for him, why are you living a nightmare that you're not telling anyone about? Or is it because you don't have the people who would wake up to pray if they knew what was going on?

Having people like that around you can literally save your life. A study found that experiencing three or more incidents of intense stress within a year (serious financial trouble, being fired, a divorce, etc.) triples the death rate in socially isolated middle-aged men but has no impact on the death rate of men who have many close relationships. As Rudyard Kipling wrote, "The strength of the Pack is the Wolf, *and the strength of the Wolf is the Pack.*"

The next time you experience terror by night, remember that the greatest human who ever lived did too. And he shows us the way through.

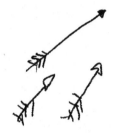

Prayer

Thank you, Father, for being my refuge and my fortress, and for paving the way in walking through fear. Fill me with strength to follow your footsteps through the darkness and into the light. Amen.

BREATHE, THINK, AND LIVE

× Do you ever feel ashamed of being afraid? How does that complicate things?

× How does knowing that Jesus experienced fear empower us?

× Refer to your list of fears (and add to it if you're so inclined). What biblical sentries or verses can you find to talk back to those terrors with an "It is written . . ."?

x Might you be leaving out any food (aka mental junk) that could attract bugs? Attract terror and worry?

x Take a moment and bring your list of fears to God with a "not my will but yours be done" approach, like Jesus did. How does knowing that almighty God is on top of your fears relieve loneliness?

x Identify your backup crew—people you can call for prayer and support. If you don't have such people, commit to pray for them to come into your life, and ask for discernment and wisdom as you purposefully put yourself deeper into Christian community. How can you begin to reach out to your people as you face your fears?

Day 25

‖‖‖ ‖‖‖ ‖‖‖ ‖‖‖
‖‖‖

A TRIP TO THE DUMP

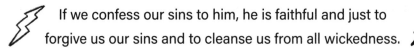

If we confess our sins to him, he is faithful and just to forgive us our sins and to cleanse us from all wickedness.

1 John 1:9 NLT

At the beginning of the year, we challenged our entire church to do a seven-day fast so we could re-center our hearts on heaven. I decided to take the week off not just from food but from buying anything online or even researching things to buy online (reading reviews, watching YouTube videos, etc.).

It was honestly more challenging for me than giving up food! I found myself constantly thinking of things I needed to buy. Little stuff like toothpaste and a new propeller blade to replace the one that broke on my drone. I hadn't realized how compulsive online shopping had become, even though we had a garage full to the ceiling with empty Amazon boxes.

The day I could no longer get into the garage, I finally decided to do something about those boxes. I put an audiobook on, put on my headphones, grabbed a box cutter, and went to work cutting them down. Then I filled up every square inch of my SUV and took them to the giant recycling receptacle at the dump. It took two full trips. (You know you have a problem when . . .) Afterward I paraded my entire family around the garage, exclaiming how happy I was to have our lives back.

A couple of weeks later, though, I was shocked to see the boxes already piling up again. So I cranked up another audiobook and got busy. Since then it has become an every-other-Sunday ritual for me.

I don't know why, but I find it to be cathartic. There's just something so satisfying about getting rid of garbage. It makes me feel like a new person. The purge hits reset on my mind.

The truth is that we all need to undergo a similar kind of purge on the inside—regularly. We accumulate gunk and grime and shame in our hearts and minds just from being alive. And we need an outlet for all that junk. This is why regular confession is such an important part of our relationship with God. As we sin and are hurt and get offended and offend others, the garages of our hearts get filled with trash and boxes and hurt feelings and regrets. If we don't have a place to take those things, they pile up and cause us harm. (Plus we don't have any space left to receive the new things God wants to give us.)

Without a regular purge, your soul will quickly become overrun with the stinking thinking and rotting feelings that accumulate over time—things like fears, discouragement, anger, and jealousy.

To be clean you must come clean. And the only way to come clean is to bare your heart before the Lord. In essence, it is a trip to the dump for your soul.

If you are going to function at the level God wants you to, taking out the emotional and spiritual trash needs to become a daily part of your life. The Holy Spirit is the one who shows you what things need to go and takes them away when you confess them.

This spiritual trip to the dump is what Jesus had in mind during the Last Supper when he washed the disciples' feet. The disciples had been arguing about who was the greatest, and right there, right then, Jesus modeled true greatness for them by stooping to serve them.

Peter objected, saying that he would never let Jesus touch his feet. Jesus responded, "If I do not wash you, you have no part with Me" (John 13:8).

Peter relented and said, "Lord, not my feet only, but also my hands and my head!" (v. 9). Never one to do something halfway, Peter went from being unwilling to have his feet cleaned to wanting a full-body sponge bath!

Jesus politely declined and said, "He who is bathed needs only to wash his feet, but is completely clean" (v. 10).

The word for "wash" here is not the one for bath; it describes a spot cleaning. In that day, it was customary to take a bath and get cleaned up before going to someone's house or to a feast. But because people wore sandals, when they walked the dirt roads, their feet would get dirty. When they arrived, they would be clean except for their feet. Only their feet would need to be washed to restore them to a fully clean state.

On a spiritual level, Jesus is describing two distinct washings: one done once to become thoroughly clean, and the other done as needed on an ongoing basis. The first washing takes place when you become a Christian. Titus 3:5 says, "Not by works of righteousness which we have done, but according to His mercy He saved us, through the washing of regeneration and renewing of the Holy Spirit."

Salvation is more powerful than any cleaner on the market today. Better than Tide, OxiClean, Comet, Scrubbing Bubbles, or even bleach. Jesus washes us clean from our sins with his blood, the only cleaning agent that can do the job, so effective it only needs to be done one time.

The second washing is a spot cleaning to take care of the daily things that get on us, that come from walking in a dirty, wicked world. Our hearts have been scrubbed, but we can still get defiled from anything that accumulates: fears, thoughts, movies, conversations, websites, and so on.

Our souls need to be cleansed from these kinds of things on a daily basis with a regular trip to the dump. As with cleaning any stain, time is of the essence; the longer it sets, the worse it gets. Otherwise the caked-on gunk hardens and calcifies.

This principle is sound when it comes to just about every area of life. In your finances: don't let the receipts get crazy; balance the books often. In your health: many do crash diets, P90X for a few months, then nothing; better to do a little every day. So it is with your soul: daily attention is the best way to roll.

Don't rely on a weekly spiritual booster shot, such as going to church on Sunday to fill your tank so you can coast the rest of the week. Stains will start to set in. Use a Tide-pen approach.

Here are four ways to let Jesus daily spot clean your heart.

I. SPEND TIME WITH HIM IN HIS WORD

Psalm 119:9 asks, "How can a young man cleanse his way? By taking heed according to Your word." When was the last time you opened your Bible? God's

Word will feed the right wolf in your life (goodness, honesty, purity) and starve the wrong one (your fears and all the things you fight).

2. PRAY AND TALK TO HIM THROUGHOUT THE DAY

You can honestly talk to him anywhere about anything. He's right there. Simply take off the mask. Stop the pretense. Stop hiding. Come clean. It feels so good to be forgiven, and it allows you to be authentically you: broken but loved, marred but chosen, heavyhearted but being healed. You can't be healthy and whole without unburdening your heart before the Lord.

3. LISTEN TO WORSHIP MUSIC AND PODCASTS

We live in amazing technological times. Even when you're commuting, you can experience digital discipleship. If you get into it, you'll be excited for traffic because you'll be able to finish a whole message or keep singing along with your favorite worship band.

4. SERVE AT YOUR CHURCH

When you find a place in your local body of believers, you'll be more likely to stay on mission and fight off the lethargy that comes from sitting around too much. It will also keep you from being a consumer at your church and turn you into a contributor.

Each one of these strategies will help you keep the garage of your heart unclut-tered. Don't just close the door on it and let it turn into a hoarding nightmare. Open the door, face it head on, and let God do his cleansing work.

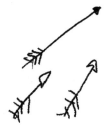

Prayer

Father, I give you all the cluttered, burdened, secretive, messy corners of my heart and ask you to cleanse them. I won't rely on anything else but your healing power to do the hard work in my soul. Amen.

BREATHE, THINK, AND LIVE

× Think back to when you identified some stinking thinking or junk thoughts that attract fears and darkness. How can you get motivated to take that to the dump?

× How is avoiding confession of our sins like avoiding our fears? Why do we not have to worry about fear of failure when it comes to confessing our sins to God?

x After Jesus has washed us once and for all, he's still there for a spot clean. What kinds of things accumulate on you on a day-to-day basis that need to be sponged off? Where do they come from?

x What are the advantages of doing this daily rather than periodically?

x How can you practically make a confessional trip to the dump a part of your daily routine? Make a plan for folding these things into your life:

— When and how will you spend time in his Word? In the book itself, through Bible apps, through streaming it, and so on.

— When can you check in for quick prayer throughout the day? Rather than depend on your fears as they come up to trigger prayer, take advantage of regular events such as commutes, coffee breaks, or even setting reminders on your phone.

— Do some research on podcasts and worship media to start feeding your ears.

— How can you serve more in your church and community?

Day 26

|||| |||| |||| ||||
|||| |

USE WHAT YOU'VE GOT

His divine power has given to us all things that pertain to life and godliness, through the knowledge of Him who called us by glory and virtue.

2 Peter 1:3

My brother bought me a MoviePass card that allows me to see a movie in the theater every twenty-four hours. It sits there in my wallet whether I see any movies or not. The same is true of gym memberships. Just because you have the right to go to the gym and freely utilize the equipment doesn't automatically mean you get a six-pack. You have to walk in and take advantage of what your membership gives you access to.

So it is when it comes to the arsenal of power at your beck and call as a child of God. We are not to wage war against things like fear, sin, and darkness according to our own resources. The power that leads to victory is not in us or from us; it is with God and comes to us from his hand. But that same power has to be wielded. Having it and using it are two completely different things.

Today's verse from 2 Peter 1:3 makes a big promise. Do you feel like you really have "all things that pertain to life and godliness"? Potentially you do, but practically you have to tap into what belongs to you, one moment at a time.

Paul made a similar statement: "Blessed be the God and Father of our Lord Jesus Christ, who has blessed us with every spiritual blessing in the heavenly places in Christ" (Ephesians 1:3). Are you thinking, *Wait a minute, I have "every spiritual blessing in the heavenly places in Christ"? Where are all these blessings?* They are at the same place the biceps and abs you wish you had are—waiting for you to take advantage of your gym membership. They won't work if you don't work them.

One of the biggest mistakes you can make is to try to do God's work without God's power. There's a great scene in *Iron Man 3* where Tony Stark's autopilot malfunctions, and he flies hundreds of miles out of the way, crash-landing in snow-covered Rose Hill, Tennessee. Feeling claustrophobic, he ejects. But then once he realizes how brisk it is in the snow, he wishes he had stayed in the coziness of the suit.

He trudges through the snow, pulling the Iron Man suit behind him like a kid with a sled. He is totally huffing and puffing as he slowly pulls it one foot at a time. It's a perfect visual because the suit wasn't designed to be carried by him; it was designed to carry him as he executed his calling as a superhero.

The Bible says we are *in Christ*. Remember, "in Christ" is a theological term to describe the way God sees us as being completely covered in Jesus. But when it comes to fighting battles, you can also think of being in Christ the way Tony is in the Iron Man suit. Through our continued reliance on Jesus, we tap into an arsenal of protection, ammunition, and navigation.

So many Christians are struggling to pull what should propel them, trying to fight the battles of this life with their own strength, waging war according to the flesh. Don't make that error! Stay in the suit. Jesus is not something to carry like a religious trinket or a good-luck charm; He is a risen Lord who will carry you. Call for fire support, and when God makes the ground shake with energy, be ready to occupy the territory he has cleared.

So what exactly is this fire support, you ask? There's a great description in 2 Corinthians 10:3–5: "For though we walk in the flesh, we do not war according to the flesh. For the weapons of our warfare are not carnal but mighty in God for pulling down strongholds, casting down arguments and every high thing that exalts itself against the knowledge of God, bringing every thought into captivity to the obedience of Christ."

Most ancient cities had a fortress, a stronghold, on top of a hill, in which its residents could take refuge. A stronghold provides many benefits. For one, you can see the enemy coming, so it's harder to be taken by surprise. For another, you have light on your side, because the enemy has to look up into the sun to see you. When someone else has an elevated position over you, though, you are a sitting duck, an easy target.

In your life, a stronghold is an area in which you have become entrenched in believing something that isn't true or in doing something you shouldn't be doing. As a result, the Enemy has a heavily fortified position in your life. Simply put: it's a constant pull in the wrong direction.

These strongholds can take many forms: fear for one, but then there's pride, anxiety, lust, resentment, jealousy, bitterness, condemnation, shame, physical abuse, substance abuse, addictions, jealousy and covetousness, eating disorders, compulsive behavior, and low self-esteem. The list goes on and on.

These strongholds put a chokehold on the joy, growth, freedom, and strength you are meant to experience. They neutralize your effectiveness and lock you in a state of darkness and arrested development. This much is for sure: you'll never experience all that life holds if you're living with strongholds. They're like having a blockage in your arteries. No matter how hard your heart pumps, you just can't get the necessary blood flow to your body.

Are there things constantly pulling you in the wrong direction? Here's how to demolish them:

1. Spot them. *Ask God* to open your eyes to hidden sins so you can identify them and recognize them for what they are: areas of oppression in which sin has barricaded itself and the Enemy has a power position against you. We are all blind to our own blind spots.
2. Renounce the thinking or behavior and set your soul against it. This is called repentance.
3. Paint the target so heaven can blast it with God's supernatural power. (More on this in a sec.)
4. Let your squad in on what has been going on. God alone can forgive, but other people are needed to walk with you in your healing (James 5:16).
5. Vigilantly and diligently build something in place of the sin so it can never be rebuilt. If you don't follow up your new start with a new plan, the stronghold will be taken again, and it will be seven times worse than the first time. Getting triple-bypass heart surgery is only effective

if the patient exercises and follows a low-cholesterol diet afterward. Otherwise he ends up right where he was before the surgery.

Let me expand on the third step—paint the target. It's like letting a fighter pilot know where to drop the bomb and agreeing on a code word you can say when it's time to let it rip. To do this effectively you need to use precise language. Every mission has a clear code word used to authenticate commands. In *Black Hawk Down*, for example, the word was "Irene."

We, too, have been given a word, and it is a name. Philippians 2:10 says, "At the name of Jesus every knee should bow, of those in heaven, and of those on earth, and of those under the earth."

You can force your enemies to their knees by being willing to kneel on yours. As the old hymn put it, "Satan trembles, when he sees the weakest saint upon his knees."

We can face the inevitable battles of life by using prayer as the weapon that turns off darkness. And as you pray, make sure you use the right word. The name of Jesus—not just a generic God or the man upstairs—is what gives us power. It's completely available to us; all we have to do is use it.

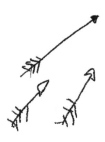

Prayer

Thank you, Father, for offering all things that pertain to life and godliness. Break down the things in my life that are keeping me back from stepping into this promise. I want to grab hold of all that you have for me. Amen.

BREATHE, THINK, AND LIVE

× What are the dangers of trying to slog through this process of freedom on our own?

× Why is it important to stay "in the suit"?

× Is anything stopping you from fully believing the promise that you have everything you need in the power of Christ? If so, what's at the bottom of that?

× How is it a relief knowing we war with God's power, not ours?

× By now, you've probably started to identify some strongholds in your life. They might have to do with your regular fears, things that always bring you to your knees. Or maybe they're bad actions, habits, or flat-out sins that are a constant pull in the wrong direction. From our journey thus far, what jumps out at you as the top strongholds you're warring against?

× For each of them, go through the steps we outlined today.

1) SPOT: Ask God to open your eyes to how this is affecting you in your blind spots.

2) RENOUNCE: Say no to that stronghold and resolve to act against it.

3) PAINT: Slap a bull's-eye on the target and pray in the name of Jesus.

4) CALL: Bring in the squad. You need them as much in your strongholds as you do in your fears. Keep those connections strong.

5) BUILD: What could replace this stronghold? What's your new plan to build on the mind space this thing used to take up?

Remember, this is all done with Jesus' power. Stay close to him and use the code word (his name) whenever you need to.

EVERY MISSION
HAS A CLEAR
CODE WORD
USED TO
AUTHENTICATE
COMMANDS.

Day 27

THE BEST DEFENSE IS A GOOD OFFENSE

 The reason the Son of God appeared was to destroy the devil's work.

1 John 3:8 NIV

When you begin to get your heart right, don't be surprised when the Devil doubles down. Why? The Enemy of your soul sees good things happen and he gets nervous. So he lets out a roar.

When I was a freshman and had just given my life to Jesus, I went through a period so dark that I was sick to my stomach with thoughts of self-harm. It wasn't that I wanted to kill myself; I just had thoughts that told me I was going to.

One night when I was home alone, I couldn't shake the thought, *You're going to kill yourself.* I tried to pray, in an attempt to ask God to help me. Finally, I called one of my youth group leaders and told her what was going on.

"I feel like a dark force is smothering me with thoughts about death at my own hands, and I don't know what to do. I'm terrified right now, like the Enemy is just going to chew me up." I began to sob. So many times I had wanted to tell someone but felt like I couldn't or that it was admitting I had done something wrong. Sharing those fears with another person was the most wonderfully relieving thing ever.

The leader immediately sensed I was under spiritual attack. She spoke words overflowing with life about me and my future and prayed for me. Then she gave two scriptures to me and told me to memorize and repeat them over and over again whenever those kind of thoughts surfaced:

- "You will keep him in perfect peace, / Whose mind is stayed on You, / Because he trusts in You." (Isaiah 26:3)
- "I call heaven and earth as witnesses today against you, that I have set before you life and death, blessing and cursing; therefore choose life, that both you and your descendants may live; that you may love the LORD your God, that you may obey His voice, and that you may cling to Him, for He is your life and the length of your days; and that you may dwell in the land which the LORD swore to your fathers, to Abraham, Isaac, and Jacob, to give them." (Deuteronomy 30:19–20)

Giving me those verses was like giving a lifeline to a drowning man. For years, they were my go-to defense when I was under heavy attack.

Around that time I also discovered how to use worship music to control the atmosphere around me. I discovered I couldn't go to sleep without listening to my favorite worship song. My youngest daughter, Clover, struggles with nightmares these days, and she has found comfort by singing "Tremble" by Mosaic MSC to herself while snuggling her black blankie.

Thoughts can't be erased; they have to be replaced. You have to create a new track to your life's soundtrack and let that be praise. Let that be worship. Let that be faith, not fear, because fear is faith in the Enemy.

When you face fear, remember this: when the devil messes with you, it's a mistake on his part. Because every time he fights against something, he's tipping his hand so you can see what matters to him.

The only reason the Enemy would come against you is because he sees value in you. The only reason he would try to force you to think something like *I'm worthless* or *No one wants me on their team* or *I'm never going to win* or *I stink* is because it's not true, and he wants to throw you off the trail of your God-given greatness. *Father of Lies, there is no truth in him.*

It's because you're precious that he tries to make you feel worthless. It's because you're meant to choose life that he would try and suggest you should choose death. Whatever he says, it's the opposite, because he's a liar.

If Satan tells me he's going to give me everything in a moment so I can have instant gratification and not wait for God to give me what he wants to give me, I'm not going to listen. If he tells me to take a shortcut, I'm going to take the long, hard road instead.

The devil opposes what he's afraid of. *So let your fear help you sniff out what he's trying to snuff out. Let it be a diagnostic tool to determine your calling.*

Run *toward* the roar! Rise up and do exactly what the devil doesn't want you to do. Refuse to go gently into the night. Don't be taken without a fight. In

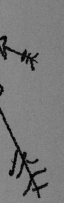

RUN
TOWARD
THE
ROAR!

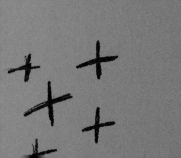
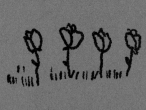

jujitsu, you use your opponent's force and energy against him. Likewise, when you experience terror during the darkness, become a source of terror to the kingdom of darkness. It's terror-jitsu.

I have said out loud, "It seems the Enemy doesn't want us to do this. We must be on to something. So we'll not only do that, but we will also do this other thing too."

You're chosen. You're loved. You're called. You're equipped. You're meant to show life to people who are hurting. You're meant to encourage those who are weary and give the bread of life to those who are hungry. You are meant to pioneer and create and lead and design and invent and sing and dance and write. You will fall and get back up again and learn from your mistakes and grow wise and strong and brave. When your time here on earth is done, you are meant to leave a legacy that will ring out through the ages and touch thousands into eternity.

When the Enemy tries to come at you to smother you, rise up in faith and do whatever he's trying to get you not to do with twice as much resolve and ten times the determination, relying on the power of the Holy Spirit. When you're full of anxious thoughts and worry and spiritual warfare and peer pressure from the world, and your mind feels as though there are squirrels running around inside it, don't back down; double down.

Don't just discard the strongholds and idols that Jesus gives you the power to wage war against. Melt down what has been torn down and turn it into ammunition so you can fire it across enemy lines.

You can do this. It won't be easy or fast or pain free, but you can do this.

A boxing instructor once explained the difference between a cross (in which you hit hard with a straight punch) and a jab (in which you throw a fast, light punch that is more distracting than damaging). She said something that I think will put steel in your spine and propel you forward in the fight: "The jab keeps them busy, but the cross is your power."

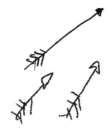

Prayer

Father, renew and strengthen my mind. Replace the lies and fill my heart with the truth of your Word. I choose to keep my mind on you so I can walk in your perfect peace. Amen.

BREATHE, THINK, AND LIVE

x Now that we know the Enemy has tipped his hand, revisit your fears and your strongholds.

x Knowing what you know, how are these things exciting?

x Use your new diagnostic tools. What are the opposites of all these fears and strongholds?

x Do any of them light you up inside? Do they seem like a calling? How can you possibly double or triple down on these opposites?

x Reload on Scripture, worship, prayer, and community. You have so much ammunition. What role will you give these things in not only defending yourself but playing offense by building something new?

Day 28

HOPE HAS A ROPE

 This hope we have as an anchor of the soul, both sure and steadfast, and which enters the Presence behind the veil, where the forerunner has entered for us, even Jesus, having become High Priest forever.

Hebrews 6:19–20

My wife, Jennie, and I both have anchor tattoos. Mine's on my chest, and hers is on her forearm. We got them fourteen days after our daughter Lenya's departure to heaven. Lenya loved anchors. She had an anchor T-shirt she often wore. She used to have an anchor necklace, but it had been misplaced (as just about everything in our home inevitably is at some point in the course of a normal week). When we chose Lenya's outfit for the burial, we ransacked the house but couldn't find the missing anchor necklace. Her older sister, Alivia, volunteered an anchor necklace of her own.

The whole celebration of Lenya's life had an anchor theme to it. Google "Lenya Lusko Celebration" and you can not only see the anchors but also hear for yourself Alivia, who volunteered to speak, talk about Lenya. (Interestingly enough, that video has been viewed more times than any message I have ever preached.)

It's perfect actually. The symbol of the anchor is powerful because of what it stands for: hope.

And hope is a powerful thing.

Of all the battles we've been talking about, perhaps the most important battle is the one you fight within your mind and heart to not give up. To keep moving forward, facing those things you must deal with. That's not just a theory, it's a fact backed up by medical science. Meg Meeker observed, "Physicians can often tell the moment a terminally ill patient gives up hope. Death comes very quickly afterward."

So what is hope? At its most basic level, to have hope is to believe that something good is going to happen. That help is on the way. That it's not over yet. And that no matter how dark it seems, there's going to be light at the end of the tunnel.

Our hope is a living hope, because we have a living Lord.

The thing about anchors is that to be effective, they must be attached to something. There is always a connection: a rope or a chain. They aren't wireless and can't be connected by Bluetooth. That connection is every bit as vital as the anchor itself. It doesn't matter how securely that big hunk of metal is wedged into the ocean floor—if you're not tied to it, it's not the least bit helpful. The chain matters greatly.

The wonderful thing about the anchor of the soul is that it, too, comes equipped with a mighty chain. Hope has a rope: the Holy Spirit.

Before entering God's presence in the ascension, Jesus promised to send his Spirit to be our helper (John 14:15–31). He is our great rope that cannot be frayed, the one who has lashed our hearts to heaven. Through the Spirit we have an everlasting guarantee, a down payment on the life that is to come. He is the proof that there is more in store and that death is not the end.

In times of overwhelming fear or darkness and weariness from fighting, your anchor should strengthen you, but you should also be encouraged by the chain.

This was a total lightbulb moment in the initial twenty-four hours after Lenya went to heaven, in the single darkest and most frightening day of our lives. Lenya is with Jesus and—through his Spirit—Jesus is in me, so there is a direct connection between Lenya and me. In a very real sense, my family and I are holding hands with the one who is holding Lenya.

To help our daughters see through Lenya's lenses, to see how we're connected to heaven right here, right now, we would actually act out this idea as a family. I had Alivia stand around the corner in our hallway, where we couldn't see her, and we pretended she was Lenya. Representing Jesus, I straddled the corner, holding her hand and Jennie's and my daughters Daisy's and Clover's hands. "Though you guys can't hold Alivia's hand or see her, you are directly connected to her through me," I explained. This chain analogy gave us great peace and alleviated the "my child is lost in a grocery store" panicky feeling Jennie and I often felt. In our fear, we had a rope to grab onto.

Until we see Lenya in heaven, we are connected with her through the Holy

Spirit. Through choosing to be filled with God's Spirit, we can feel the cord grow taut. Honoring Jesus and walking in the light help reel it in. The more room we give the Spirit to come upon us and control our lives, and the more receptive we are to heaven's signal and guidance, the greater peace we will enjoy. Our fear fades, and we can run forward.

On the other hand, giving in to temptation and choosing to sin puts slack in the line. So how do you get the slack out of hope's rope? How do you feel more connected? You must be filled afresh with the Holy Spirit. The more we are filled with the Spirit, the more heaven comes near.

There are lots of ways to grow in your relationship with God's Spirit: serving other people, taking a walk and venting to the Lord, reading the Bible, talking to a friend you can be real with. But I have found that there is nothing so powerful and effective as gathering together with the church. When we come together, brick by brick, we are more the house of the Lord than we are alone. His Spirit dwells there in power, and he inhabits our praises. We gather so we can glow and then go.

These moments are like little safe harbors, sanctuaries from pain and fear. For those brief moments, suffering isn't welcome and has no choice but to flee from the power of Jesus Christ. In his light, we see light.

We have shed more tears and received more strength at church than maybe in any other place. I have looked to the floor and seen a puddle of tears at Jennie's feet more times than I can count. When I look up, her hands are raised, and she is locked into the glory of the Lord, taking heart and renewing her courage.

My friend Carl Lentz told us, "It's better to win ugly than to lose pretty. The secret is to keep showing up." There is real truth to that. Don't quit! Scream if you need to scream. Cry if you need to cry. But don't let go, because you are going to need what God wants to give you.

It is also crucial you don't wait for a crisis before you get these sorts of rhythms in place. You must train for the trial you're not yet in. The worst time to try to get ready for a marathon is when you are running one.

We made the decision as a family to plant ourselves in the house of the Lord before the bottom dropped out, and as a result, we had the root systems in place when we needed them the most. Satan wants us separated from the group so we are easier to pick off. During the Dust Bowl of the 1930s, many people fled the affected areas and headed to places like California, as depicted in *The Grapes of Wrath*. A group called the Last Man Club resolved to not leave no matter what. Their motto was, "Grab a root and growl." I love that! As we as a family have made the difficult decision to dig our claws in and commit to the local church, we have experienced great power from the pack. By God's grace, we're still rooted and we're still growling. And you can too!

Right now is the time to strengthen your faith. Today is the day to put down roots in a local church. Sing your guts out to the Lord as a drowning man cries for air, even when you don't feel your need for him. Open your Bible and seek God's face each morning, on the days you don't get anything out of it and the days when the verses jump off the page. Have family devotions with your kids regularly. Mix it up. Take a prayer walk together or do a prayer dance. Don't wait. Do it today.

Public victory comes from private discipline. If you are willing to do the hard work now, then when the dark days come, you will be ready. Keep your anchor on a short leash, and when fearful times come, you'll have the strength to move forward without being lost at sea.

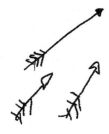

Prayer

Thank you, Father, that because you are a living Lord, I have a living hope. Draw me into deeper waters of trusting you and believing that, even in darkness, I'm not alone.

 BREATHE, THINK, AND LIVE

- x How would you describe your relationship with the Holy Spirit—God living within you?
- x How does knowing you're connected to Jesus through the rope of the Holy Spirit give you hope?
- x How is hope the opposite of fear? Of your particular fears?
- x How is hope deadly to strongholds? And your particular strongholds?
- x In the separations of life, between earth and heaven, and even between us and the version of ourselves that we know God made us to be, how does hope become essential? How does it connect us to the goodness of God?
- x How are all the weapons and tactics we've discussed this week really ways to tighten your connection to the Holy Spirit?
- x Think of your roots in your local church. If you have them, how can you strengthen them? If you don't, how will you commit to planting them and winning ugly rather than losing pretty?

WEEK 5

BE tHE DIFFERENCE

Day 29

HHT THL HHT HHT
HHT IIII

STAY IN THE PACK

Just as each of us has one body with many members,
and these members do not all have the same
function, so in Christ we, though many, form one
body, and each member belongs to all the others.

Romans 12:4–5 NIV

In the first week of this journey, my goal was for you to see that you're not
ordinary. God has destined you for impact. There are great things he wants
to accomplish through you. My prayer for you has been that as you begin to
shift your vision with these new lenses that your eyes would be opened to
see your greatness in Christ. You have a unique and powerful voice, and as
long as you have breath in your lungs, there is a microphone in your hands.
Every day you have a choice of how you are going to use this platform you
have been given.

What's not a choice, though, is that we need people to make this happen. This is not a solo act. You were also made for community.

Many of us tend to shrink back from community, especially when we're struggling with pain, fear, or darkness. But we've learned that when we decide we're done being ruled and pushed around by the Enemy, when we're ready to become a victor instead of a victim, instead of shrinking back, we find that power like a wolf rises in us.

We touched on the awesomeness of wolves in Week 3. It's not just because they are powerful and smart and have big bad teeth and claws. They have some really endearing qualities, too, that we would do well to learn from.

Let's consider the fact that every wolf has a pack. Wolves are social creatures. It's one of the fascinating things about them.

Read this excerpt from *The Wisdom of Wolves* and tell me if you don't find yourself wanting to channel your inner wolf:

They care for their pups with a familiar devotion and share our reflexive instinct to care for youngsters, related or not. They hold a place in society for their elders. They push boundaries and explore, then return to visit their families. They care what happens to one another, they miss each other when they're separated, and they grieve when one among them dies. . . . They are benevolent leaders and faithful lieutenants, fierce mothers, nurturing fathers, and devoted brothers; they are hunters, adventurers, comedians, and caregivers.

To be a wolf is not just to be a brave warrior; it is also to be a loving nurturer, and that is your destiny.

And a wolf pack—that protective, organized force of nature—is part of your destiny too.

It's amazing to observe the way wolves organize themselves. It's a bit like an army. Of course, we all know that wolf packs have leadership. You can't get a lot of people together without them agreeing on a pecking order, without them agreeing on the harmony that's going to come, just like an army has generals and captains and all the rest.

The most notorious wolf in the pack is the alpha wolf. But did you know that every wolf pack has an alpha male and an alpha female? God intended leadership for both of them—both sexes. So lest you be envisioning a stereotypical alpha male here, ladies, there's more to this story. God wants you to see yourself as strong, as brave, as capable in his hands, as daughters of the King, as daughters of the light. There's strength in that.

And of course, there are beta wolves too. When I was researching this, I learned beta wolves function like the lieutenants. There can be a whole bunch of beta wolves in a pack. They serve to keep the peace and keep everybody else in line, implementing the alpha's directives.

There are even more positions. At the other end of the spectrum, you have an omega wolf. The omega wolf gets to eat last. You'd think the omega wolf would feel lower than, less than, but it turns out the omega wolf provides an important function for the pack. He basically keeps morale up. You might say he's always cracking jokes. He functions like a court jester and keeps things going relationally. I love that, because, much like in the body of Christ, God gives different gifts to different people. There's a place in the pack for everybody. Whether God's calling you his lieutenant or omega or alpha or something in between, there's a place for you.

LIFE IS
BETTER
TOGETHER.

Sticking together not only makes for a better wolf pack, it makes for a better life for us as well. Simply put, life is better together.

But we have to ask ourselves, *Who are the people in the pack that I'm rolling with? Who am I doing life with?* Give serious thought to this, because it's been said you are the average of the five people that you are closest to. I think that's true. It makes sense if you're going to do life with people, you're going to end up where they're going.

My friend Craig Groeschel likes to say, "Show me your friends, and I will show you your future." If you want to become fascinated with something, hang out with people who are interested in that thing. And if we want to fight like wolves and take back our lives, we have to do life in cooperation with other people who are going to push us on in our love for Jesus, in integrity, in bravery, and in community. The pack is indispensable.

That's why churches that employ small group ministries are so effective. At your church it may be called a community group. At my church, Fresh Life, we call them Fresh Life groups. They are people who say, "Hey, we want to get together once a week or once a month, whatever life allows, and pray together and encourage each other. And in between, we'll text each other and be in a Facebook group together and share verses that are helping us out. We'll offer to babysit each other's kids, or we'll have each other's backs at school."

It's hard when you feel like you're the only Christian around. It's nearly impossible to live a fulfilled life alone. But with your pack, you'll get the support you desperately need when you need it and encouragement to live out your calling.

Jennie and I both have looked back at our spiritual journeys and have said we are who we are because of the small groups we were in, from high school to this very day. Being part of the pack is not just a necessity; it's a gift. To make your difference, to live your story, you're gonna need your pack beside you.

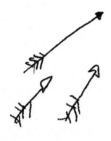

Prayer

Thank you, Father, that you created me for community! I'm grateful that you've given me the gift of friendship and relationship, and that this pack is where I learn more of who you are. Bring people into my life who will draw me closer to you. Amen.

BREATHE, THINK, AND LIVE

× What are the dangers of going it alone, of being a lone wolf? What protection does the pack provide?

× What kinds of things cause you to shrink back from community? How can you run toward them?

× How is your platform directly tied to other people?

× Do you see yourself as a nurturer? What kinds of things are you uniquely equipped to nurture in others?

× Which people need your nurturing? How can you put yourself more in contact with them?

x If you are in a church community pack, how do you perceive your position in that community? Not as a way of ranking from alpha to omega, per se, but to reinforce what you bring to the pack.

x Do you think of your contribution as valuable?

x If you were to shrink back from the group, what might be lost?

x Think of the five people you're closest to. In what ways are you an average of them? How would you describe the direction you are going in together?

x Do you want to raise your average? How could that be done?

x Think about the health of your pack right now and the pack you'll need beside you if you are going to live out your destiny. In what ways can you strengthen your bonds and have each other's backs? For Christian community in particular, how can you encourage each other?

Day 30

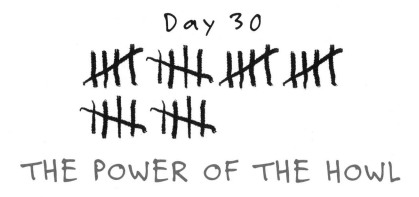

THE POWER OF THE HOWL

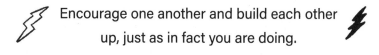 Encourage one another and build each other
up, just as in fact you are doing.

1 Thessalonians 5:11 NIV

What makes a wolf pack work? What bonds them and allows them to function? What keeps them healthy and alive? It's all about communication. If we're going to run with a pack, communication is key.

When you think of how a wolf communicates, you probably think of that bone-chilling howl they are so famous for—that *a-rooo* on your Halloween soundtrack. But did you know that when wolves howl, they intentionally achieve something called dissonance?

That basically means they're pitchy on purpose. When wolves howl, they don't harmonize. They actually avoid harmonizing. Why? Because it makes them appear more numerous than they really are.

If every wolf in the pack attempted to harmonize, you'd only hear their one united sound. But when they howl with dissonance, you can't tell if there are five or fifty. It makes them sound more numerous than they are. When they're all howling with their own unique pitch, it works for the strength of the group.

Earlier I mentioned the book *The Wisdom of Wolves*. It's written by Jim and Jamie Dutcher, two researchers who spent six years living with a wolf pack. That's commitment. That is dedication.

They lived among the pack so they could learn their ways and write about them, creating the most extensive study of life in a wolf pack ever conducted. According to the Dutchers, howling is not the only way wolves communicate. They also communicate with things like scent and body language. And they're constantly interacting with each other not just through howling and facial expressions but also through touching. It's how they affirm their family bonds. They stay united because of the ways they communicate.

Like a wolf, you communicate nonverbally too. In fact, experts estimate that a very small percentage of our communication occurs through the words themselves. The great majority of what we say each day involves what we do with our bodies, our facial expressions, and the tone with which we communicate. (This turns out to be pretty problematic when we do a lot of communication via text and email. it can lead to a lot of reading between the lines, for better or worse.)

As you interact with others, you hold incredible power to affect them, to bring life and not death to them. Think of it this way: God loves the people in your life so much he put *you* in their lives. And he gave you means to communicate with them so they could be better off because they encountered you. He gave you your brain and the power to choose your words and actions so you could represent him to them.

Pretty powerful thought. Sobering too, because if Jesus is the Lord of your life, then he should be the Lord of your lips. Colossians 4:6 reminds us to "let every word you speak be drenched with grace" (TPT). Grace is unmerited favor, by the way. Grace is not ever deserved. This is so important, because the people God is blessing through you, these people in your pack or in your trajectory, they are not going to be perfect. They might even be infuriating. When you open your mouth, let it be in a way that reflects God by giving grace.

What makes grace into grace is that it is undeserved. Have you ever been tempted to use your words to tear someone down? Instead, try allowing the way you speak to drench them with something that they don't deserve. Something that they're unwilling to give. Something they probably desperately need.

Let your words be drenched with grace. And then "tempered with truth and clarity" (Colossians 4:6 TPT), because there is a time for speaking hard things. There's a time for different conversations. There is time to tell someone, "Hey, what you did hurt me." There is a time to say, "I love you so much. And just between us, as friends, here's something I think is holding you back. Take it for what you will." I'm not saying there's not a time for that. We're not just going to walk around like saccharin little elves, you know?

The author of the book *American Wolf* explains that the alpha wolf often uses the howl as a way to get the members of the pack worked up and excited before going out on a hunt. It's like they're rallying each other with, *Here we go. We've got it. We're going to kill the deer.* This type of howl often follows "an exuberant display of affection in which wolves leap on one another, forming a furry pile of tail-wagging bodies." If that's not adorable, I don't know what is.

But it makes me wonder: Do the people in your life feel like you are in their corner? Do you use your words to speak life in a way that puts the wind at their backs? That reminds them of who they are and whose they are? Do the words from your mouth make them believe the best is yet to come, that God is for them and not against them, and that he has a good plan?

I wonder if God has given us our words so we might encourage each other toward good works. It is a hard world and people are going through difficult stuff. *You're* going through difficult stuff.

If wolves have the common sense to do something to work themselves up before they face the fray, maybe we should consider doing the same. Why wouldn't we get excited, physically support each other with a fist bump or a high five and verbally encourage each other? Speak truth over yourself, over your family, over your friends. Speak faith over your day. Give some time to the preparation before facing the world together. Remember these truths and say them out loud:

"God loves you."

"You're his prize."

"He cares about you."

"You're the apple of his eye."

"He's got plans for you."

"He's got your name written on his palm, so don't you speak bad about someone who's written on Jesus' hand."

When your words are full of faith, impossible things can happen. Let your goal be to use your words in such a way that they bless the heart of God, inspire faith in those around you, and cause a ripple that will ring out into eternity.

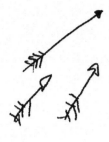

Prayer

Father, teach me to call out for help when I need it and to be a help to others in their time of need. I believe you placed me perfectly in my sphere of influence. Allow me to be used by you to strengthen the pack. Amen.

 BREATHE, THINK, AND LIVE

x What are some of the most affirming words someone in your community has ever given you? How did they strengthen your bond?

x How do you and those closest to you encourage each other on a daily basis? What's most encouraging about your communication? Least encouraging?

x When has someone given you grace in their communication? When have you seen it in action? How is it powerful?

x What's the value of saying hard things with grace? What's the hardest thing someone's said to you that you've appreciated?

x Think of your circles, your pack (or packs), your daily interactions. Where do they need to rally?

x Today, and for the days that follow, target specific people in your pack and send them a howl by text, a quick word, a note—anything. Determine which words of life you're going to speak to them. Put a reminder on your calendar if that helps. Use some of the words above or words from quotes or scriptures or words tailored to that person and situation. Whatever you do, start the howl, and see how the group is strengthened.

Day 31

IHT IHT IHT IHT
IHT IHT I

DON'T KICK THE BEEHIVE

There is one who speaks rashly like the thrusts of a sword,
But the tongue of the wise brings healing.

Proverbs 12:18 NASB

Maybe you'd say to me, "Levi, I'd love to make a difference in people's lives, to use my story to help others, to encourage them, but honestly I'm just not that good with people. I'm not a people person. They wear me out. I open my mouth, and things don't go well. I'd rather just leave this community thing to someone else."

To which I'd say, I feel you. People are messy. Anytime we try to build relationships and live our calling in a world full of humans, conflict will happen. Thankfully, though, we can set ourselves up for better interactions by learning to manage ourselves.

Let me explain how I know this. It's possible we haven't met before, so I'll give you the intro: "Hello. My name is Levi Lusko, and I am bad at managing myself."

Do you ever do things, say things, or tweet things only to realize that what you got is not what you wanted from that exchange, that interaction? Yeah. Me too.

I don't want to fight with my wife. I want to laugh with her. I want her to be happy. I want us to have adventures and inside jokes and tickle fights and get old together like we are a real-life version of the couple in *The Notebook*. Then why do I act like a jerk or say things that hurt her feelings or lose my temper and huff around like a five-foot-ten-and-a-half-inch toddler who hasn't gotten his way? I don't enjoy being in conflict with her. I'd much rather we were making love or dreaming about the future or taking a walk or praying or eating pasta.

I don't want to fight with my dad. I want to drink coffee with him, work out at the gym with him. Laugh about travel antics. Reminisce about old stories that make us smile. Why do I say things that push his buttons? Why do I get defensive and indignant? It's not because I wanted us to be at a stalemate. I'd prefer we were laughing until one or both of us were crying or planning a way to get together and have fun.

I don't want to fight with those I work with. I want to work hard with them, not against them. I want our workplace to be one where failure isn't disciplined but expected and embraced, so long as it is born of initiative and innovation. I want us to be swept up in passion and excitement and laughter and feel drained but thrilled by the end of the day. So why do I channel my inner petty dictator and become a mercurial, stormy, demanding boss? Why do I bring Evilevi to work? I'd much rather my staff were confident in which boss they would get whenever they encountered me rather than have to tiptoe on eggshells until they find out which version of me they are meeting with.

In all these situations, I speak words, make decisions, and give off non-verbal cues that take me further away from where I actually want to be. They separate me from the people I love and the people I serve. They separate me from my pack. If I could tell when this was happening, I would course correct. But it often doesn't sink in until Evilevi has already made a mess and left me with the bill.

Dale Carnegie said, "If you want to gather honey, don't kick over the beehive." If a bee stings you while you're gathering honey, choosing to respond by kicking the beehive isn't going to help the situation; it's going to make it worse. Beekeepers use slow movements and smoke cans to calm the bees they want to receive honey from. Instead, a gentle hand will help you get what you want (Proverbs 15:1).

Listen to the results of an eye-opening experiment described in the book *Everyday Emotional Intelligence*:

> Participants who were treated rudely by other subjects were 30% less creative than others in the study. They produced 25% fewer ideas, and the ones they did come up with were less original. . . . We saw more sparks from participants who had been treated civilly.

You don't even have to be the recipient of the rough behavior; simply *witnessing* incivility has negative consequences. The same study showed that "people who'd observed poor behavior performed 20 percent worse on word puzzles than other people did."

The bottom line is that rudeness causes performance and team spirit to

BEING RUDE IS NOT CHEAP; IT'S EXPENSIVE.

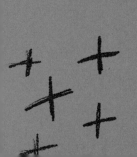

deteriorate. There is a cost to being rough. It may get you what feels good in the moment, but it will be at the expense of what you actually want. Being rude is not cheap; it's expensive.

Deep down, you know this. Even while you are sassing your parents, being sarcastic with your spouse, or spouting off at the customer service person who is high on condescension but low on customer service, you know you are making the problem worse. But in those moments, you don't care. You just want to kick the dang beehive.

Proverbs 30:32–33 advises, "If you have been foolish in exalting yourself, or if you have devised evil, put your hand on your mouth. [That right there is some good relationship advice.] For as the churning of milk produces butter, and wringing the nose produces blood, so the forcing of wrath produces strife."

The forcing of wrath in a relationship is, every single time, going to lead to strife. And you're thinking, *Of course. Ugh. Obvious, right?* And yet why do we walk away surprised when people's noses are bleeding—ours and theirs—and act mystified as to what happened? *I can't believe it. I can't believe it. I ca—How did this happen?* Oh, I don't know, you were violent and aggressive and mean. You forced your wrath. But now you don't like the outcome?

In those moments, we usually say to ourselves, *Well, that wasn't my intention.* Right? It's nothing but a big fat excuse, because you wanted to do what you did. We simply use our intentions to make an excuse for our actions.

But here's a beautiful, life-changing truth: your intentions don't matter; your behavior does. No one can hear what you wanted to say; we hear only what you said. *The impact you have on the world is what you're accountable for.*

When you allow yourself to be provoked, you give up the one thing that is yours and yours alone: control of yourself. You see, if I can get to you, I become the boss of you. If I can say the right combination of words to make you lose your cool and Hulk out, I am effectively in charge, because you've given me the password that unlocks your bad behavior. How many times are you going to let people get your goat before you start locking your goat up in a different place?

I get it. Trust me, I do. I have triggers that have successfully ticked me off so many times it isn't even funny. When I feel unloved or off-kilter or bombarded or out of control, it is almost too easy to allow something to upset me and make words come out of my mouth that I don't want to speak. I feel hypnotized by my hurt feelings, so I fly off in a rage I know I will regret. I have had my emotional passport punched from visiting that territory so many times that I've run out of pages.

But I'm done. I'm sick and tired of handing the reins of my life over to other people and circumstances. I've found freedom in realizing that regardless of what someone else does, I still have a choice and can respond in a way that is completely different than my initial impulse.

If I'm responsible for the impact I have on the world, I'm going to have to be responsible for my behavior toward people, right? The difference between people and animals (yes, even wolves) is that, because we were made in the image of God, we can choose not to do what we feel. We can choose something better. We can choose something in line with our callings, our identities, and our greater purposes toward others. We can back up our good intentions with solid actions and manage ourselves for the good of the pack.

Prayer

Father, align my behavior with my intentions. Fill me with your spirit so I can foster rich, regret-free relationships, and choose the path that will stir up peace. Amen.

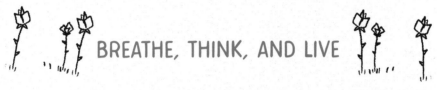

BREATHE, THINK, AND LIVE

- Who do you fight with who you don't want to fight with? How does that start?
- What tends to push your buttons? Why do you tend to want to push other people's buttons?
- Think about a time you were treated rudely. What was the aftermath of that? How did it affect you then and even now?
- Think about a time you were rude to someone else. What was the fallout? For you? For them, if you know?
- Now, how about a time you *witnessed* rudeness. What did that do to the general vibe? To you personally? To the aggressor and the recipient?
- This may sound obvious, but it's important to drill it in: In what way does rudeness affect your pack's morale? What does the recovery time look like? What could you be doing with that time instead?

x Think about a time you had good intentions but ended up forcing wrath. What happened to those good intentions?

x In what situations could keeping yourself from being provoked leave you with the upper hand? What are the benefits to this?

x If you are responsible for the impact you have on the world, what kinds of choices can you make in dicey interactions that will preserve that impact? Or strengthen it?

Day 32

FOUR SQUARES FOR A BETTER YOU

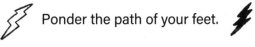 Ponder the path of your feet.

Proverbs 4:26 ESV

Our culture places a high value on being true to ourselves. Not doing and saying what we feel like is hard because it flies in the face of that concept. But consider this: carefully choosing your words and responses leads to something even better—becoming who you want to be.

My friend Lysa TerKeurst puts it this way in her book *It's Not Supposed to Be This Way*: "If we are going to be true to ourselves, we'd better make sure we are being true to our most surrendered, healed, and healthy selves, the ones God made us to be."

You might struggle with anger, but you are not an angry person. You might struggle with people, but that doesn't make you not a people person. That doesn't mean you weren't made for community. You were created in the image of a triune God. Those things you feel are not who you really are.

I've come up with a four-part matrix that helps me manage myself when things get dicey with other people. It's a graphic that you can copy onto a cocktail napkin, a scrap piece of paper, your journal, or whatever you can get your hands on. I highly recommend that the first few times you use it, you physically draw it and fill it in, because it will force you to cool down. Eventually, you'll be able to do it in your mind in real time, and it will give you the freedom to keep from saying everything you feel like saying.

To begin, draw a cross, and in the top quadrants, from left to right, put the words "Analyze" and "Extrapolate," leaving a good amount of space below them. In the bottom quadrants, write the words "Prioritize" and "Navigate."

ANALYZE

Under "Analyze," write "I want to . . ." and then write exactly what you want to say or do because you're angry, sad, or rejected. Don't run from your emotions; study them.

- I feel like saying something mean or snarky.
- I feel like throwing a tantrum.
- I feel like breathing fire on this customer service person's judgmental self for not helping us, even though we have been waiting longer than anyone.

As you write down what you want to do, really try to feel the tidal wave pushing you to those behaviors. Don't fight it; just feel it.

Do this every time you feel ready to do something that's going to result in strife. Then stop and analyze what you want to do and why you feel like doing it.

Over time you'll begin to notice common threads, consistent themes, and patterns. You'll notice, *Every time this happens, this is how I feel, and this is what it makes me want to do.* The more we can understand the emotions that drive our words, the better chance we'll have to process them before we act on them and before they affect our relationships.

In his book *Anger*, relationship expert Gary Chapman wrote, "Almost all research now indicates that the venting of angry feelings with such aggressive behaviors does not drain a person's anger but actually makes the person more likely to be explosive in the future." The pen is mightier than the stress doll.

EXTRAPOLATE

After you've analyzed the situation, the next step is to extrapolate: if I do this, then this will happen. Play out the scenario and take it to its logical end.

It's like running a simulation, like having Iron Man's virtual assistant inside your head. The point is to understand the trajectory. *You can fly that high, but just so you know, you don't have enough power in your suit to land safely, Mr. Stark. So go for it if you want, but just know it's going to be a bumpy landing.* It's incredibly helpful to understand the implications of a given decision before taking action.

If I say this, she will say that. What's going to happen next? What is he likely to do? What am I then going to do? How will that escalate the situation? What will it do to the tension? What are the long-term impacts on my family, on my kids, on my reputation, on my career?

Just get it all out there. You still can choose to take that course of action. Just make sure you do so with an understanding of what will happen next. Ask "Will this path take me to a place I like? Will I enjoy the frosty silence that comes from having responded with a comment that stings?"

A wise person observed, "If you speak when angry, you'll make the best speech you'll ever regret." The great thing about extrapolating is that you can size yourself up and grab the reins of your emotions before they rush you toward a chasm.

PRIORITIZE

The third step is to prioritize. Write "What I really want to happen is . . ." You played out the implications of what you wanted to do and (I hope) realized that is not what you want to end up with. Now ask, if you were to come up with the storyboard for this situation, what's in the last pane of the comic? What is the final scene before the credits roll?

- I want to be heard.
- I want a seat on the plane.

- I want respect.
- I want to end the night laughing with my wife.

When I take the time to do this exercise, I realize there are things that matter much more than temporary vindication. As good as it feels to unload on someone in the moment, the pleasure is extremely short-lived, and you're left with a mess. Don't trade what you want most for what feels good right now.

NAVIGATE

The last and most important step is to navigate. In this quadrant, write "What I need to do to get there is . . ." Pro tip: it will often be the opposite of whatever you started out feeling like doing.

- To get the table at the restaurant you want, try kindness and empathy, not sarcasm and condescension.
- Honesty, humility, and vulnerability work when you want attention from your spouse.
- Calmly telling your sister she hurt your feelings works better than burying the pain deep down and letting it come out through passive aggressive digs.
- Ask people you're in conflict with to help you see the situation through their eyes instead of assuming that your perspective of the event is correct and definitive.

The Bible agrees that gentleness and friendliness are stronger than fury and force: "A gentle response defuses anger, but a sharp tongue kindles a temper-fire" (Proverbs 15:1 THE MESSAGE).

Understanding these four steps and applying them has helped my marriage immensely. Our old tendency was to do whatever we would have come up with in quadrant 1. But things change by quadrant 4. It's when you humble yourself as a servant that people want to follow you as a leader. Being nice is one thousand times more effective than being a jerk.

In situations when Jennie was feeling neglected, she used to lock down and pretend everything was fine, but her body language clearly showed she was not happy. What she wants is kindness and affection and attention, but she was trying to get it by acting like a porcupine—and no one wants to hug a porcupine. The best way to get me to care for her is for her to lean in and tell me she is sad and needs me. That breaks my heart and makes me want to embrace her. The other strategy confuses and frustrates me and pushes me away.

Focusing on where we want to end up makes us more likely to communicate better, plus we spend less time trying to hash out conflicts that could have been avoided. Choosing to abandon the decision to scold, nag, belittle, and criticize will feel so good when you navigate to where you prioritized that you want to be.

Another helpful question to consider is this: How would the person I want to be handle this? You might think that is a little ridiculous, but it helps. I'll think, *What does the Levi I wish I were say to his wife or kids when he is frustrated?*

More often than not, the answer is more listening and less speaking, more empathizing and less sermonizing. No one cares what you know if they don't know that you care. When I think it through like that, my choice is easy: get thee behind me, Evilevi!

In the quest for a better you, picture who you wish you were and imagine that person irritated. Then choose to respond as he or she would. Ask God for strength and close the gap between who you are and who you were born to be. You'll never be sorry you made the right choice, regardless of how it feels in the moment.

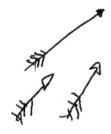

Prayer

Father, teach me to ponder the path of my feet. Teach me to slow down, to respond instead of react, and to close the gap between who I am and who you created me to be. Amen.

BREATHE, THINK, AND LIVE

x Here's a test graphic for you. Think of a recent time you wanted to lay into a member of your pack, and fill this out as practice.

ANALYZE

EXTRAPOLATE

PRIORITIZE

NAVIGATE

× Analyze: I want to . . .
  - What do you feel like doing?
  - What are the emotions behind that?
  - When it comes to feeling those emotions, what makes you want to avoid those feelings? What would happen if you let them hit you instead?
  - How do you feel after writing them down?

× Extrapolate: If I do this, then this will happen . . .
  - How will this escalate?
  - What are the long-term and short-term impacts on
    • my family?
    • my kids?
    • my reputation?
    • my career?

× Prioritize: What I really want to happen is . . .
  - What's the ideal ending? What do you want for you? For them?
  - Would you trade that ending or outcome for the satisfaction of a swift kick?
  - What are the benefits of not kicking the beehive—that is, the honey, so to speak?

× Navigate: What I need to do to get there is . . .
  - What's the opposite of what you wanted to do in quadrant 1?
  - How do things look different when you see the situation from their eyes?
  - What would the best version of me do here?

Day 33

||||| ||||| ||||| |||||
||||| ||||| |||

RISE HIGH, BOW LOW

But friends, you're not in the dark, so how could you be taken off guard by any of this? You're sons of Light, daughters of Day. We live under wide open skies and know where we stand. So let's not sleepwalk through life like those others. . . . Since we're creatures of Day, let's act like it.

1 Thessalonians 5:4–8 THE MESSAGE

When I was researching wolves, I learned that observers can tell how success-ful a wolf will be in life by the way it carries itself. Isn't that crazy? A wolf's carriage opens a window to see who's going to be able to (1) get into a strong pack, (2) form a new pack, and (3) get the prey/be successful.

There's almost a nobility to the bearing of an alpha wolf, even when they're little cubs. Observers look at little things like the tail to tell them what's going on in the wolf's life. I like to think these researchers are out there with their binoculars, like "Oh, no. Bob's tail's down. He's having a bad morning. He must have eaten a bunny instead of an elk."

Much can be discovered about the wolves' identities, mood, and position of power just by watching them. Observers check out what they are communicating with their ears (being up or down) and their fur (being bristled or not), whether they show their underside as a sign of submission, or if they participate in a sparring match, jostling for power.

It's the same with us, when you think about it. When you carry yourself in a nervous way, hunched over, slumped and looking at the ground, you're essentially hiding your sensitive underbelly. You're saying to your pack, "Please don't gut me. Don't you dare slit my throat." Not exactly the best start for making strong connections with people.

I used to preach while stressed. It used to just wipe me out. I'd end up dry heaving like Eminem in the bathroom before his rap battle in *8 Mile.* I'd be walking around backstage hunched over trying to protect my underbelly. Turns out I was doing the exact opposite of what I needed to do.

If you haven't seen Amy Cuddy's TED talk titled "Your Body Language May Shape Who You Are," you should check it out. She talks about how nervous energy usually causes you to hunch over, tuck your chin, put your hands on your neck, or cross your arms. But that cascades into more nervousness because of the release of cortisol (stress) into your system.

However, putting your hands on your hips, like Wonder Woman, or up in the air, is the universal sign of victory and celebration. When you do this, your body releases testosterone, and your levels of cortisol drop by as much as 25 percent. This can happen in as little as two minutes.

I was shocked when I initially watched this video, but the first thing I thought of was the book of Psalms. It is *full* of commands to praise God with raised hands and heads held high. You can't find a psalm that tells you to tuck yourself into a ball and meekly sing to God with your hands in your pockets. It's all about shouting with a voice of triumph. Could it be that part of the reason God wants you to shout and sing triumphantly with your arms in the air isn't just because of what you are declaring about him but because of what happens to you when you obey? He gives you feelings to match what is coming from your lips and modeled with your body.

That's one of the many reasons why you will not find me backstage during the worship set before I speak, as I was in my early days. I need the time with my church family, worshipping through song, more than I need a few more minutes cramming. So I'm right out there with them, because I need the physical *and* spiritual posture of worship and victory in my life if I'm going to serve God, and his people, well.

I also read that wolves communicate to their pack through fine-movement facial expressions, like ears forward for joy or eyebrows raised for fear. What does your face look like right now as you read this? Is your brow furrowed in concentration? When Jennie sees me deep in thought while reading stressful emails, she will often smooth out the skin between my eyes right above the bridge of my nose, as if to say, "Lighten up, buddy." She is giving good advice in terms of both what kind of response you radiate and what you will receive in response.

Researchers have found that people respond in kind to the facial expressions they encounter. A smile is met with a smile, a frown with a frown. This mirroring happens subconsciously. We instinctively reflect what we see. If you want people around you to cheer up, there is something you can do about that. Seeing someone display facial expressions of fear, anger, sadness, or disgust causes an increased heart rate, elevated skin temperature, and sweating. Your face can absolutely have an impact on those around you, for better or worse.

Like your posture, your face can affect your own mood. Smile and you'll eventually feel better. Your body doesn't know why you are smiling or carrying yourself like a prize fighter; it just senses you are and responds appropriately. Try it. It might feel weird at first, but when the stress melts away into confidence, you'll be glad you did.

Now, I hear your objection: *I can't show that kind of zeal if it isn't how I feel, because that wouldn't be real.* Let me warn you that this kind of thinking is why so many marriages fall apart and why so many people never experience the breakthroughs God has for them. People who do the right things *only when they feel them* never enter into the victorious life. Worship is not a feeling expressed through actions; it's an act of obedience.

Today's verse says, "Since we're creatures of Day, let's act like it" (v. 8 THE MESSAGE). We act like it—even when we don't feel it—because of our identity in Christ. Because of who we are. That comes first. We choose to act in a way that reflects who we know we are: creatures of the day. A royal priesthood. That's not fake at all.

Here's one more wolf thing that blew my mind: when wolves enter a den, they slide in on their bellies through the hole; then, researchers say, no matter which wolf they are—beta all the way to omega—they always do a small bow before the alphas. It's a posture thing. It's a deference thing. It's an honor thing.

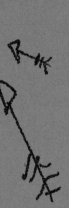

LIKE YOUR POSTURE, YOUR FACE CAN AFFECT YOUR OWN MOOD.

If the wolf served in our military, the bow would be the equivalent of a salute with respect.

But get this: evidently no wolf in the entire pack bows lower than the omega. The omega wolf bows lowest of all.

When I heard that, I couldn't help but think about Jesus, who said, "I am the Alpha and the Omega. I'm the first and the last. I'm one who was and is. I am the Lord Almighty" (Revelation 1:8, author's paraphrase).

For us, Jesus' death on the cross triggered life through our salvation. And though He was Lord of all, Alpha of all, he gave that away and lowered himself to become a man. And not just any man—the lowest. As a servant, he died even the death of the cross, and it's that death that triggered life for us.

My encouragement to you, as an individual and in your pack, is to live a life bowing low before Jesus, the Alpha and the Omega. You realize so much power when you get your posture right—when you let your life be marked by worship and surrender to God—because bowing down makes you poised to rise up.

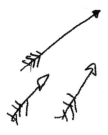

Prayer

Father, grow me in humility so I can be like Jesus. I know your desire for me is victory and strength; bring me to my knees so I can rise up in power. Amen.

 BREATHE, THINK, AND LIVE

x How would you describe your physical posture when you're around people? Pay attention today to the signals you're giving. What are they?

x How do you think those signals affect people? How have you seen this in action?

x Think of someone who you know and admire who has good bearing. What do they do?

x How does it affect people? What kinds of reactions do they typically get?

x Think about your facial expressions. In what ways can you go from "back off" to "welcome"?

x Think back to the work we did surrounding your identity and calling. In the posture of your body and your heart, what do you think a noble bearing would look like? What do you think its effect would be on yourself and on others?

x Watch the Amy Cuddy TED talk and experiment with the Wonder Woman position. What do you find?

x Think about your most stressful moments. How was your posture? Inside? Outside?

x How do acts of worship bond us as a community? How do they make us healthier in body and soul?

x What does Jesus' posture tell us about his nobility? How do we relate to him in this way?

x What can you do going forward to help you mind your posture in all ways?

Day 34

TWO STEPS TO THE LEFT

This is the word of the LORD to Zerubbabel: Not by might, nor by power, but by My Spirit, says the LORD of hosts.

Zechariah 4:6 ESV

There's a walking path I frequent when I'm studying and I hit a brain block. I find I pray better walking. I think better walking. It's just rejuvenating to my spirit. I get to zone out and just stroll.

A little while ago on one of these walks, I snapped back to reality and noticed I was walking in a strange fashion, almost like I was playing hopscotch. I realized I was being careful to avoid all the little gifts that had been left on the path by a flock of Canada geese that visit the area. But the amount of poop was insane that day. At a certain point there was almost no exposed pavement. I don't know what kind of deranged party they were having, but if any Canada geese are reading, you need to know that I do not want an invitation.

Yet I persisted. Let it never be said that a Canada goose ever got the best of me. I almost had to do the splits with each step, like Will Ferrell going up the escalator in *Elf.* I finally got to the end of the path and turned around only to realize, *I've got to do this all over again.* I was disgusted, plus I already nearly had a charley horse.

As I began to take careful steps, I looked to my left and noticed a green, grassy belt running parallel to the path. Apparently it had not been pleasing to these geese. It was completely clean, completely open. I felt pretty stupid as I realized the entire time I had been walking through the land mines, I could have been walking on the grass. I took two steps to my left, and from then on it was poop-free all the way home.

I think that illustrates the difference between trying to live for God and letting God's life live through you. It was a tiny change—just two steps to the left—and I went from awkward flailing to smooth sailing.

Maybe you're making every effort to build your relationships, to live in your community and be a blessing to people, but it feels like you're walking through a poop minefield. Don't despair. It might not be that you need a huge change to achieve significant forward progress. You might be moving in the correct direction, just making it harder on yourself than you need to. You might have been walking a path strewn with what the apostle Paul said he learned to count as "dung," namely, human efforts (Philippians 3:8 KJV). Once he learned to rely on the Spirit's power, he still gave just as much effort, perhaps even more.

God's grace never makes you want to do less; instead, you are open to going above and beyond, because you know it's no longer about you.

Perhaps the shift from self-power to Spirit power will be like taking two steps to your left and going the same direction you were before but now seeing God dramatically bless your efforts.

That's the message God gave to Zerubbabel in the Old Testament book of Zechariah. (If you don't know where that is, here's a pro tip: find Matthew, the first book of the New Testament, and go two steps to the left.)

God called Zerubbabel to rebuild the house of God. It was dangerous and risky and difficult, especially without walls to protect them. When they asked God how they could possibly be safe without walls protecting them from invasion, God told them, "I will protect you, not with walls of wood and stone but with a wall of fire!" (Zechariah 2:5, author's paraphrase).

That was enough for Zerubbabel, so he and his crew got to work. They worked for almost nine years, but after nearly a decade of labor, they had almost no progress to show for it. They were met with opposition, barriers, discouragement, and unforeseen problems. And of course there were fights and division, because let's face it, you can't accomplish anything great without criticism and hardship. Every day they were trying and trying and trying, and it was just not working, not working, not working.

It makes you feel for Zerubbabel. It's hard enough to keep a team motivated and on track and fired up when you can point to visible success. "See what's happening? Look what we got to do. How many of you know we're going to do more of this?" But for nine years, they had no progress to be encouraged by.

His wheels were spinning in the mud, and he couldn't get any traction. This is when doubts creep in: *Maybe I'm not the guy. Maybe I'm not cut out for this. Maybe we should leave it to someone else.*

Zerubbabel fell into an emotional funk, but God spoke to and quickened his heart and, through an angel, gave Zechariah a vision for Zerubbabel. Zechariah saw a golden lampstand with seven flames fed by a never-ending supply of olive oil straight from a self-pressing olive tree. It was an eternal fire, perpetually burning and completely self-sustaining.

The vision came with the following instructions: "This is the word of the LORD to Zerubbabel: Not by might, nor by power, but by my Spirit, says the LORD of hosts" (Zechariah 4:6 ESV).

Game changer. This was the missing piece: secret power. Now he would be relying on God's strength instead of his own. A tiny tweak would create an enormous difference, because he wouldn't be trying to soldier through or grit it out to make it happen. Instead, he was going to take two steps to the left and get into the lane called grace.

By relying on God's strength, he would be able to fulfill God's call. Trusting in the Holy Spirit, Zechariah and the people did the impossible. "Mountains were made plains before them, and the final stone was put in place with shouts of 'Grace! Grace!'" (Zechariah 4:7, author's paraphrase).

Perhaps the word of God to Zerubbabel is the word of God to you too. Are you at your wit's end in your marriage? On your last nerve with your kids? Running on empty at work? Maybe you are trying to do the right thing but relying on your own power, which results in spinning your wheels.

Ask the Spirit to shift you two steps to the left. There are amazing, re-markable things God wants to do with the people in your life on your college campus, at your place of business, and in your neighborhood. But first you need to ask Jesus to breathe on you and give you his strength. And you will need to do it again tomorrow, because power is perishable. The minutes don't roll over.

You can't win the war within without asking God every day to energize your efforts and then being sensitive to the cues he gives you along the way. Like the rumble strip on the side of the highway, God directs us through gentle nudges to correct our courses.

No matter what God calls you to do, his command comes with enablement. For instance, if you join the air force they don't expect you to bring your own F-16; they give you all you need to fulfill your orders.

You also don't need to understand how you're going to complete your mission. You just need to do it in obedience. The end result will be that you see God magnificently work things out. But first you have to take the gutsy step of faith that says "I believe."

God has the power; you just need to ask for it. He is a good Father. He won't give you a tarantula if you ask for a Fruit Roll-Up. But he will give you the Holy Spirit if you ask him to. Try it. And when you get the wind knocked out of you, ask for a second wind and a third and a fourth. If you're knocked down seven times, he'll give you a seventh wind too.

Prayer

Thank you, Father, for the promise of your power and strength. I choose today to rely on you, to tap into your grace, and to believe in you to energize my efforts. Amen.

BREATHE, THINK, AND LIVE

- x In your relationships, are there any areas you're over-relying on self-power to make things better—that is, any areas you're feeling drained, hopeless, or discouraged?
- x How can relying on the spirit in these situations change things?
- x Reflect on the attitude "It's no longer about you." When it comes to your pack and the people in your life, how could this attitude spur you to do more instead of less when things get tough?
- x Think about poor Zerubbabel and his crew. Have you ever had an interpersonal situation where you were laboring and nothing was working? How would you invite the Holy Spirit into that situation? How could you be more open to his leading?
- x Think about the cry, "Grace! Grace!" Pray and ask the Spirit to bring his grace and power into every area of relationship in your life. How might it change things to take two steps toward him?
- x What are the Spirit's rumble strips in your life and relationships? How can you be more sensitive to his getting you back on course?
- x How will you signal yourself to turn back to the Spirit again and again?

Day 35

𝍷𝍷𝍷𝍷𝍷 𝍷𝍷𝍷𝍷𝍷 𝍷𝍷𝍷𝍷𝍷 𝍷𝍷𝍷𝍷𝍷
𝍷𝍷𝍷𝍷𝍷 𝍷𝍷𝍷𝍷𝍷 𝍷𝍷𝍷𝍷𝍷

PENCILS DOWN

 You do not know what will happen tomorrow. For what is your life? It is even a vapor that appears for a little time and then vanishes away.

James 4:14

I can't think of any two words I associate with a terrible feeling in the pit of my stomach more than the phrase "Pencils down." It is the sound of a hundred tests I wasn't prepared for. I don't know what you did when teachers said that, but I know what I did. I tore through the remaining questions, filling in as many bubbles as I could: C, C, C, C, C, C, C, C . . . I figured one out of four was better odds than zero out of four!

But here's the truth of it: life is a timed test. We're all living against a deadline. The Bible tells us that a moment is coming when God will say "Pencils down" to each of us: "It is appointed for men to die once, but after this the judgment" (Hebrews 9:27).

You might be surprised to know that the origin of the word *deadline* actually has something to do with real dying. In the early 1900s, it was a physical line painted on the ground around the inside of a prison, measured out twenty feet from the walls. If prisoners crossed this line, they would be shot on the spot. It was literally a line of death.

But really, that's how life is. At a certain point we cross a line, and it's all over. But none of us knows where that deadline is. It's invisible. Sand keeps falling from our hourglasses, but there is no way to know how much we started with or how much we have left. We may have an appointment with death, but it's not on our Google calendars.

Life really is like a vapor. This is true for us, those we love, and those we are meant to impact. We must live each day all the way to the hilt, because each day could be our final one here. Death could show up at any time, and it often doesn't call ahead.

Before Lenya went to be with Jesus, when I thought of death, I would focus more on leaving earth than on going to heaven. But what I have become aware of is that death is not just a departure; it is also an arrival. I used to fatalistically think about my exit, but now, more than ever, I am focused on my entrance.

Life here on earth is not all there is. There is a hereafter. When we leave this world, we get to go home. And the way we live here has a direct impact on what we experience when we arrive there.

I began this journey telling you that you are destined for impact. There is greatness inside of you. Unlimited potential. A holy calling on your life that would make you tremble if you could fully understand. But then we discovered

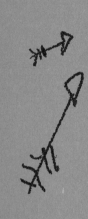

POTENTIAL
IS
PERISHABLE.

that there is a price you will have to pay to activate your calling, and the devil will do anything he can to keep you from hitting your full stride.

I want to add to this a vital word of warning: potential is perishable.

Potential has a short shelf life, an expiration date that is approaching. Your calling isn't a Twinkie. Like milk or produce, it won't keep forever. It can spoil and go bad. These works God wants to do in your life? If you don't seize them, they can pass you by. You have a limited amount of time to act on the plans God has for your life before they are out of reach.

This is a timed test. There is a deadline. God is going to say, "Pencils down." And anything you don't tap into by the time this life ends shall remain undone forever.

This is why Jesus said in John 9:4, "I must work . . . while it is day; the night is coming when no one can work."

There are things you can do on earth that will be impossible one minute after you die. Bringing comfort to the discouraged. Feeding the hungry. Sharing the gospel. These are all things that will be impossible to do in heaven, but they can be done right now.

My daughter's life ended the night before the world was supposedly going to end. There was all that hoopla about the Mayan calendar and how December 21, 2012, would be the earth's last day. But they were wrong. The world is still spinning, but Lenya is not on it anymore. People talk a lot about the end of the world, but the end of your life might come first.

What this means is that time is limited, and so the devil will do anything he can to keep you from sensing the urgency that will mark your life if you wake up each day knowing it could be your last. He won't try to talk you out of doing the things you are intended to; he'll simply tell you to put them off.

One of his biggest lies is "You can do it tomorrow." He knows what you need to know: there might not be a tomorrow. Today could be your one and only chance to be kind to that stranger, tell your kids about Jesus, or invite that person to church. You need to *carpe* the heck out of this *diem*!

Make no mistake: God will accomplish all he wants to do. The question is this: Will you let him do it through you? If we won't stand up and do what God has planned for us, he will bless the person down the block or the church around the corner with the opportunity. Whenever his still, small voice calls us to do something, it's as though we are given the right of first refusal. Let's not say no. Let's give all we have to each other with the time we have left.

A thousand years from now, we won't be able to change what we did in our lifetimes, but if we do it right, we will be enjoying the fruits from it. To quote the words of Maximus Decimus Meridius from *Gladiator* (quite possibly the best movie ever made), "What we do in life echoes in eternity." I pray that no matter what life throws your way that you would honor God, give him space to move in your life, and serve him with all your heart until you stand before him face-to-face.

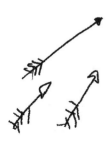

Prayer

Father, I declare war on the lie that says "put it off till tomorrow"—I want to step into the fullness of what you have for me during my time on this earth. I give you my time, my talents, my surrender; use me to accomplish your will. Amen.

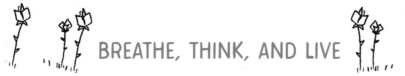 BREATHE, THINK, AND LIVE

- Has death ever felt close to you? When have you realized that your life is like a vapor?
- How might this realization empower you as you take back your life and live out your destiny in community?
- If what we do here affects what we experience in heaven, why is complacency so dangerous?
- Have you already experienced the perishability of potential in your life? How does thinking about it on a larger scale change your motivation to act?
- Think about the people in your life, in your pack, on your path, whom you can affect for the better. What can you do *right now* for them?
- If today were your last day, who would you talk to? What would you do for them or say to them?
- How can you bring that into the now?
- In what situations do you tend to put things off with people? Things like facing conflict, expressing love, giving, ministering, helping, having difficult conversations, sacrificing? What things have you ever put off that you regret?
- It's time to *carpe diem*. What will you do today that will echo into eternity?

WEEK 6

THINK RIGHT, LIVE RIGHT

Day 36

EMBRACE THE STRUGGLE

 Delight yourself in the LORD,
and he will give you the desires of your heart.

Psalm 37:4 ESV

Think about a butterfly in its cocoon. If you cut it out or help it out in any way, it will never develop the strength it needs in its wings to be able to achieve take-off. Butterflies have to struggle out in order to come into their own. Flight only comes after the fight.

The same goes for your calling. I hope I've convinced you by now that you are destined for impact. You're beloved, you are unspeakably valuable, and you were made by God for his joy and for his grand purpose. But here in this last week, you may be wondering, *What exactly do I do with all this? What's my next step?* If you are struggling with that, I'd say, "Good!" Keep struggling. Keep wrestling with it. Keep showing up every day and fighting. You'll come out of it with stronger wings.

I remember a time when I was struggling in my cocoon. Jennie and I were in our twenties and living in California, where I was following a calling to preach that I'd had since I was a kid. We were seeing exciting things happening. Plus surfing, preaching, and going to Disneyland. A guy could do worse. We could have had a happy life there. But God had other plans.

I was asked to speak at an outreach event being organized in Montana. Bob Osborne, a California businessman who grew up vacationing there, desired to see the people in the town of Kalispell come to know Jesus. So he booked some bands, rented a rodeo arena, and brought me in to speak. After the event, he told me I should move there and start a church. I assured him I would pray about it, but I didn't intend to at all.

Too honest? Sorry. It's true. I am Jacob, not Esau. Urban Outfitters, not REI. I'll take a cup of coffee and a solid internet connection over a hike through the woods. Malls, yes. Montana, no. Plus it didn't make any sense. I felt a call to bring the gospel to millions of people, and it seemed that could happen in California. I didn't even think Montana had a million warm bodies. (Unless you count deer, which I don't.)

But I couldn't get the idea of moving to Montana out of my head. It was like a splinter in my soul. I would stay up at night and think about it. And the more I did, the more convinced I became that I was supposed to go there and start a church. It was not logical. But it ate at me.

Then I started getting job offers at a few megachurches that looked, frankly, amazing. What was God doing? What was I supposed to do? I needed counsel. I needed Yoda.

I made an appointment to see the wisest person I knew, Pastor Chuck

Smith, my ultimate pastor role model. I explained my conflict: I enjoyed preaching in California and appreciated the opportunities I had there, but I wanted an adventure, a venture in faith. I wanted to launch out into the deep and let my nets down. After describing my confusion, I waited for him to tell me God's will for my life. He refused to do so. He simply said, "Levi, people need Jesus everywhere. There is no wrong answer."

I don't know if I left more frustrated or relieved. But in time I saw the wisdom of his response. Had he told me what to do, I probably would have done it or at the very least put a lot of stock in his opinion. By forcing me to make my own decision and hear God for myself, he was helping me to develop the muscles of my faith that I so desperately needed.

We decided to move to Montana. We'd give it five years.

Once I announced we were going, a number of people went out of their way to talk us out of it. Someone told me, tongue in cheek, "You do know you're planning on moving to a part of the country where it is so cold that cows die there in the winter. They just drop dead, frozen solid." *Cows die there.* His words rang in my head. What was I thinking?

One person I respected said, "It is not God's will for you to go." That got my attention. Over pancakes he looked me in the eye and said, "Levi, we need you here. There is a generation that is dying and going to hell by the truckload right here. Your ministry is effective here. You can't go." I couldn't argue with him, but all I knew was I felt as though I would be disobedient not to move to Montana and preach the gospel.

It is hard to describe what it's like to leave sunny, always-seventy-five-degree Dana Point, California, and arrive in Montana in January, a month when it's always winter and never Christmas. It reached fourteen below zero within a few days of our arrival. It was so cold, when we were unpacking our moving truck, our Gatorades froze in the bottles—between sips.

What had I done?

At our first service, fourteen people showed up. The temperature outside was fourteen degrees Fahrenheit. Fresh Life was born.

Now, thirteen years later, we have seen over twenty thousand people come to know Jesus through our weekend worship experiences and outreach events. The original church plant in Kalispell has grown to thirteen churches, spread across four states, with more being dreamed about. We were reaching huge numbers of people on TV and many more online every week. I thought I was walking away from so many possibilities by moving to the wilderness, but God blessed my willingness to embrace obscurity and lay down everything I had.

Looking back, it is easy to see all the dots that God connected to unfold his plan. Not so much in the moment. Life in real time is messy. None of it was easy, and there were plenty of disasters at the time. It turns out, the fingerprints of God are often invisible until you look at them in the rearview mirror. Just as God's calling became clearer over time for me, if you don't get impatient, his plans will become increasingly apparent to you. Just listen to that splinter in your soul. Listen, struggle, and exercise your muscles of faith.

We treat the subject of God's will as though it were this crazy, exotic, mysterious thing, but in truth it's far less cryptic. *Discerning God's calling is about who you are becoming more than where you are going.*

Perhaps it's less about what you do and more about how well you do whatever you do. It's not something you have to sit around waiting for; it's something that's all around you, even now. It's here and it's ready, if you would just open your eyes.

We get hung up on the particulars of God's concealed will, but—assuming you are walking with him and obeying his revealed will—you can do what you want or go where you want and trust that he is the one leading and guiding through your thoughts and desires. Psalm 37:4 says, "Delight yourself in the LORD, and he will give you the desires of your heart" (ESV).

I never heard God say, "Move to Montana." I was walking with him and went on a hunch. Because I was open to his leading and guiding—although it scared me at the time—I went with it and stepped out in faith. In retrospect, I can see that his fingerprints were all over it. God goes before us and sets things up, guiding us in his providence and preparing things for us to discover. But these are things you can't see in the mirror right now. You can't see them until you look back. Just believe they will be there as you keep moving forward.

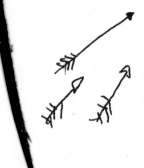

Prayer

Father, open my eyes to see what it is that you have for me, and give me wisdom on how to keep stepping closer. I trust you are always leading me and guiding me to your best. Amen.

 BREATHE, THINK, AND LIVE

x How would you describe your calling? Is it fuzzy? Clear? How are you wrestling with it?

x Look back to your reflections on week 1, "Look in the Mirror." I'm hoping you've been through a sort of identity and calling crisis that is making you think about yourself differently. How would you say that has progressed over the last few weeks?

x Do you think any differently about your identity and who you are than you did thirty-five days ago?

x If discerning God's calling is more about *who* you're becoming than *where* you're going, what calling do you see yourself moving toward as you've been changing internally? Who do you hope you are becoming? What does that mean for the actions you take?

x Describe the effect on your calling of being *in* Christ.

x Do you feel any closer to realizing your status as a genius? How might your struggle in a cocoon be honing your genius?

x Look back at day 4, at the attributes God gave you. How do those empower you to wrestle with the splinter in your soul? How do they give you the faith to dare to try something new or risky?

x How might the concept of vulnerability and authenticity keep you walking toward God's calling on your life?

x How have the words you say about yourself changed in this journey? How do you hope they change moving forward?

Day 37

STAND ON TIPTOES

For the earnest expectation of the creation eagerly
waits for the revealing of the sons of God.

Romans 8:19

If you're discouraged by the difference between who you are now and who you want to be, between the now and the not yet, think of it this way. Today is like Saturday. Yes, Saturday, the day that comes between Friday and Sunday.

In my opinion, Saturday lasts way too long. I know what you're thinking: *What are you talking about, Levi? Saturday rules! When else do we get to sleep in and ride our Jet Skis?* Let me explain.

Between Jesus' burial on Friday and his resurrection on Sunday, there was Saturday. Good Friday is famous and Easter Sunday is awesome, so we understandably think and talk about these two days most often. But in between, there is this day that doesn't get a lot of play.

That Saturday must have been a day of crushing disappointment. It was a time when promises had been made but were not yet fulfilled. Jesus had said he would come back. He had said death wouldn't be the end of the story. He had promised that if the temple of his body were to be torn down, it would be rebuilt. But he hadn't risen yet. All day Saturday, Jesus' spirit was in heaven with his Father and with the thief on the cross. But for his disciples, Saturday was filled with nothing but loss. Jesus' body lay dead, decaying, and cold. On Saturday, the rock in front of the tomb embodied the death of all their dreams, and Jesus' promise of a resurrection seemed absurd. Sunday was coming, but it wasn't there yet.

I'm sure, for the disciples, Saturday lasted *way too long*. For some of them, it was too much to handle. Why do you think the two disciples walking away from Jerusalem on the road to Emmaus had such a resigned attitude? "We thought Jesus was going to be the one. He sure showed a lot of potential. Oh, well. Party's over." The humor of the story is that they said all this to Jesus, having no idea he had pulled an Arnold Schwarzenegger: he was back (Luke 24:13–24).

We are today living in the spirit of an extended Saturday. We have a living Savior, so we have a living hope. (Yes, I know I just wrote "living" three times. Think about it.) Our life flows out of his. We can make it through our Saturday because he has promised to bring us to Sunday. God is like an elephant when it comes to his promises. He never forgets.

Jesus will come back. We will get to see our Savior's face. What the Enemy has destroyed will be restored. We will walk on streets of gold. When I readjust my lenses and remember this fact, I realize I have more life with Lenya in front of me than behind me.

But not yet. It's still Saturday. And sometimes it seems as if it will last forever.

Perhaps for those in heaven, Saturday is in Narnia time, lasting just a second, since to the Lord a thousand years is as a day and a day as a thousand years (2 Peter 3:8). Maybe when we get to heaven, it will be like going through a wormhole in the movie *Interstellar*, and we will all enter heaven's gates just moments from each other, no matter how many years apart we died. It's definitely a nice thought, but for now there are still sixty seconds to an hour. And when you are in it, Saturday lasts far too long. To borrow language from Alanis Morissette, it's "a jagged little pill."

Our third-born daughter, Daisy, is probably the most sensitive one in our house. She is sweet, thoughtful, and delicate. Not too long ago, my wife was doing devotions with the girls when the topic of problems came up. Jennie asked the girls if they had any problems they needed God's help with. Daisy blurted out her response immediately: "Well, Mom, I have a problem. My problem is that it's taking too long to get to heaven."

I feel the same way! The trouble with Saturday is that we have no clue when it will end. Jesus specifically told us that no one but his Father knows the hour or the date of his return (Matthew 24:36), and none of us knows for certain when our day will come to die, so we have to just trust that Sunday is on its way.

Until then, we groan.

Sometimes it's all we can do. When I think about Clover not having memories of her sister because she was just a baby when Lenya went to heaven: *groan*. When I see Lenya's pink bike in the garage with her helmet dangling from the handlebars and I realize I can't take her out on a ride: *groan*. When I think of Lenya not being there to be the maid of honor in Daisy's wedding: *groan*. When Alivia asks if Lenya's body still has skin or is bones like in pirate movies, a groan is the only way to deal with it. It's the sound of Saturday.

Keeping all of that in mind, read the rest of Romans 8:19–22:

> For the earnest expectation of the creation eagerly waits for the revealing of the sons of God. For the creation was subjected to futility, not willingly, but because of Him who subjected it in hope; because the creation itself also will be delivered from the bondage of corruption into the glorious liberty of the children of God. For we know that the whole creation groans and labors with birth pangs together until now.

The phrase "earnest expectation" is key. If you translate it directly, it means "to stand on your tiptoes and crane your neck." I know full well what this looks like.

All four of Jennie's and my daughters are little ballerinas. From the moment they learned to walk, they would almost constantly prance around our home on their tiptoes. I honestly can't ever remember Lenya walking flat on her feet. She almost bounced with energy and was up on her toes from the moment she woke up until she fell asleep. With the phrase "earnest expectation," Paul is saying that the whole world is so full of edge-of-your-seat excitement concerning the return of Jesus and the glory that will be unleashed that it can't contain itself from being on tiptoes in anticipation.

EARTH IS
NOT YOUR
HOME;
HEAVEN IS.

And guess what? *There is no greater help to holy living than leaning into that groaning.*

This is what will keep you going when you feel like quitting. You must make the choice to live on your spiritual tiptoes, setting your mind on things above, not on things of this earth. The future is where you must focus, not the past. When your heart is properly focused on the things that are to come instead of paralyzed by the hard and the horrible things you have had to handle, you are postured to be effective in the present.

Earth is not your home; heaven is. And when we arrive on that distant shore, we won't have to groan anymore. We will be home.

So while you're here on this earth, remember your lenses. Take a walk. Look at the stars. Watch the sunset. Turn off the TV and gather with your family in front of a fire instead. Listen to creation sing to King Jesus. Take a big, deep sigh. Let your worship and your pain swirl together and become a holy moan.

David said, "Deep calls unto deep at the noise of Your waterfalls" (Psalm 42:7). There is a sympathetic resonance that happens when the groaning is in stereo. It's not just your heart and all of creation you're hearing; the Holy Spirit himself groans in our hearts, reassuring us with sounds that can't be uttered that we belong to God and we are bound for heaven.

Lean into the groaning. And with God's help, you can turn up the excitement for all the joy and glory that await. To the degree that you cultivate your sense of longing for the next world, you will be able to combat the deadly hypnotizing pull of this one and the downward spiral that happens when we look around instead of up.

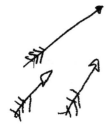

Prayer

Father, remind me every day of the nearness of heaven. Teach me to live to the fullest in this life, with the tips of my toes on the edge of eternity for the next life. Amen.

 BREATHE, THINK, AND LIVE

x How have you experienced the tension of Saturday, where you know what's broken but you've not yet seen new life? How about in the context of . . .

  – your war within yourself?
  – your relationships?
  – your work or achievements?
  – your faith?

x Think back to week 2, "Turn Off the Dark." How does our hope of heaven change the way we operate here on earth?

x How does it change the way we view our Saturdays?

x How do you feel the groan right now? How can you lean into that?

x What can you do to build a sense of earnest expectation for what's to come? How can you get on your tiptoes and cultivate your sense of longing? Consider this in the context of . . .

- praise
- simple moments in nature, observing creation
- gratitude
- letting your pain into your worship
- prayer

x How can the hope of heaven keep you from becoming paralyzed by all you have to deal with?

x In what ways has Jesus turned off the dark for you during this journey? How have you changed in your views of the eternal?

x Reflect on your views and feelings toward death. Have they evolved during this journey? How can your new lenses make you braver?

x How have you committed to keep bread and circuses from distracting you from things eternal? What do you refuse to give away?

x Have your views on the Enemy, Satan, changed at all during this journey? How does seeing under the veil affect your priorities?

x Have you seen any opportunities to use your pain as a microphone over the last few weeks?

x How does your knowledge of the war in the invisible (spiritual) inform your daily fight as you fight the war within yourself to take back your life? How does knowing your enemy and knowing who has got your back spur you on toward Sunday?

Day 38

HHT HHT HHT HHT
HHT HHT HHT III

NEVER BRING A HORSE
TO A TANK FIGHT

 You shall receive power when the Holy Spirit has come
upon you; and you shall be witnesses to Me in Jerusalem,
and in all Judea and Samaria, and to the end of the earth.

Acts 1:8

We are just about at the end of our time together. And if you're still with me, if
you've soldiered your way to this final week, then it means you are serious about
bettering yourself. In that, if you've declared war on the version of your life you
don't want to live, the version of yourself you don't want to be, you've crossed
the barbed wire. There's no going back now, my friend. Bravo!

As we've worked through all the practicalities of taking back your life, in
changing your behaviors and thought patterns, I want to remind you of one

258

critical thing. Positive thinking is important. So is watching how you speak and minding your habits. But if that is all you walk away with, then this journey is simply self-help. There is something much better than self-help—God's help. Without it, all the self-management strategies and the tips for growing your emotional intelligence will leave you powerless when it comes to true and lasting change.

It's like riding out to do battle against a tank on horseback. Seems like a really bad idea, right? But in the incredible but true story depicted in the movie *12 Strong*, that's exactly what happened. *12 Strong* takes place in the days after 9/11, when al-Qaeda hunkered down in the mountains of Afghanistan. An unbelievably brave contingent of soldiers, led by a character played by Chris Hemsworth, agreed to join forces with a local warlord who promised to get them within striking distance of the terrorists. The only problem was the Americans didn't know for sure if they could trust the warlord; there were prices on their heads from the moment they set foot in the country, and allegiances shifted every day. Oh, and they would have to travel via horseback, as there was no way to sneak up on al-Qaeda using conventional vehicles in the mountain passes.

The most jaw-dropping scene takes place when the soldiers charge onto the battlefield against machine-gun-laden pickup trucks and even full-blown tanks. The Americans had only the guns and grenades they carried with them. They would have been doomed if that were the end of the story, but they also had a laser pointer and a satellite phone. With those two vital pieces of equipment they were able to call for fire to rain from the sky. It wasn't what they brought into the battle that made them dangerous but rather who was on the other end of the phone—namely, the most powerful military in the history of mankind.

B-52 bombers circled overhead; all the soldiers had to do was mark the target with the laser and give the command by phone. He who controls the high ground controls the outcome.

It reminds me of Paul's fit of despair in which he bemoaned his inability to help himself. Remember how he said it? "I am not practicing what I would like to do, but I am doing the very thing I hate" (Romans 7:15 NASB).

If it were possible to do better on our own, we wouldn't need God. We would simply follow the golden rule, and all would be fine. The problem is that we are fallen and bent toward sinful choices. There are none who seek God; no, not one (Romans 3:10–12). If this weren't the case, God never would have sent his Son to die for us; instead, he could have just told us to be good. As a matter of fact, that was what the whole Moses on Mount Sinai thing was about. The Ten Commandments were essentially God telling us to help ourselves. It didn't even last ten minutes, and then there was a drunken orgy and a golden calf followed by complete and total anarchy.

Paul didn't finish his outburst by saying, "I guess I'll just try harder." Instead, he said, "Thanks be to God through Jesus Christ our Lord!" (Romans 7:25 NASB). Relying on Jesus is our secret weapon.

The message of the gospel isn't *try*. It's *trust*. It's what puts you in contact with power from on high. You want to talk about air superiority? There is nothing so high as the Most High. God dwells in heaven and waits to send his ultimate power in response to your asking in faith and receiving it with a mind to act on it. This doesn't make the other things we have talked about irrelevant; it makes them supremely significant. Being energized by God is like plugging into a power source. There's a night-and-day difference between using a coffee machine or a curling iron that is plugged in versus using one that is just sitting on the counter.

There seems to be a divide between those who say that God helps those who help themselves and those who insist God helps those who can't help themselves. I think they are two sides of the same coin.

It is true that salvation is all about grace. We are dead in sin, and dead people can't rise, no matter what they do. On the other hand, once Jesus has raised us from the dead, he expects us to apply ourselves effectively, working out what he has worked in us. You should pray like it is all up to God and work like it is up to you. Or to put it in financial vernacular: think like a millionaire but hustle like you're broke.

You see a picture of this when Jesus raised a little girl from the dead (Mark 5:35–43). Her resurrection was all Jesus. She added nothing to it. That is us without God: hopeless, lost, and completely unable to change our state. But once she came back to life, Jesus told her family to give her something to eat (v. 43). Why did he raise her from the dead but insist that they be the ones to feed her? God will never do for us what we can do for ourselves.

We see the same thing when Jesus raised Lazarus from the dead. Jesus was the one who caused Lazarus's coagulated blood to flow through his dried-up veins, but then he told those there to unwrap him from the grave clothes. It is God alone who can give the miraculous, but he expects you to live and take care of your miracles.

We are not to wage war according to our own resources. The power that leads to victory is not in us or from us; it is with God and comes to us from his hand. But that same power has to be wielded.

So tie yourself to Jesus, and you'll feel his power as you work out the life he breathed into you. Take off your grave clothes. And remember that when you are authentically your healed self and walk humbly as a follower of Jesus, you can live in confidence without fear, distraction, depression, anxiety, worry, regret, quarrels, addictions, darkness, selfishness, self-sabotage, narcissism, the held-hostage version of yourself you don't want to be, or anything else that gets in your way and stunts your growth. Draw a line in the sand—a crimson line painted with the blood of Jesus—and decide that the cycle ends with you. Your children don't have to inherit from you what you inherited from your parents. Fight this battle so they won't have to.

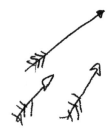

Prayer

Fill me with your power, Father. I can't do any of this on my own. Remind me of the promise of your presence when I am weak, and allow me to walk in your strength. I know that you're with me. Amen.

 BREATHE, THINK, AND LIVE

x What's your experience been with self-help? How are you finding that God's help is making a difference in the outcomes you're experiencing?

x How does it give you hope that you don't have to do all this in your own power?

x Think back to week 3, "Cross the Barbed Wire." In what ways are you, like Paul, not practicing what you would like to do yet?

x In what ways can that drive you toward Jesus?

x How are you going from *try* to *trust* in your interpretation of the gospel?

x What get-up action is he calling you toward?

x In your commitment to stop letting life happen to you and start happening to your life, what has changed in you over the course of this journey?

x How can you continue to declare war every day?

x Going forward, in what ways are you going to stop holding yourself hostage?

x How has your approach to your thinking and the health of your thoughts and mind changed during this journey? How do you hope you will continue to grow from low-level to high-level thinking?

x How has your approach to words changed? How do you hope it will continue to change?

x How will you continue to speak words of faith in your life?

x How have your habits changed? How do you hope they'll keep changing? Revisit your goals. What is going to drive you toward them?

x Look back on the concept of compound interest. What are you investing in today? In the future, what will you invest in?

Day 39

FIGHT THE FEAR

My weapons have the power of God to destroy the camps of the enemy. I destroy every claim and every reason that keeps people from knowing God. I keep every thought under control in order to make it obey Christ.

2 Corinthians 10:4–5 NIRV

One summer we took a family trip to Six Flags Over Texas. I recently came across a picture from that day and asked Alivia what her favorite ride was. Without thinking about it, she said, "Mr. Freeze."

Her answer surprised me. She had been terrified of that ride. I have never seen such fear in her eyes. For some reason she got spooked at the last minute, just as our turn came to board. I tried to reason with her. I rattled off three rides we had gone on that were worse than Mr. Freeze, but it didn't help. Fear is irrational. When I saw tears in her eyes, we bailed through the emergency exit.

Later in the day, she announced she was ready. To be honest, I wasn't completely sure she would go through with it, but she clenched her teeth, sat down, and buckled up. Blastoff! When the ride ended, Alivia had this jubilant look in her eyes that you can only get by prying joy from the clenched fist of fear. I think it is telling that in the rearview mirror the memory that stuck with her was not the ride with the most vertical feet but the one where she won a victory over herself. Facing her fears, she had run toward the roar, and she loved it.

As you keep running toward the roar of your fears and anxieties, remember that fears are irrational. They get blown up and misshapen in our minds, especially if we ruminate on them at night in our bed. Matter of fact, I'm convinced the devil works the night shift. There's just something about the wee hours where things just seem worse. Thoughts seem darker. Fears get bigger. We need to actively, continually fight by night and by day against these fears that come our way. Sometimes we do that by making choices about where our thoughts go. And other times we sit down and buckle up and take care of the practical things that feed our fears.

FIGHT, DON'T FEED

For so many people, anxiety seems to be the new normal and worry just a part of everyday life. And depression is a dark cloud that, in church circles, often has a stigma of unholiness attached to it, as though depression were somehow a betrayal of your love for God. You're not supposed to say, "I'm hurting in this way." People just want you to pray and be better. Or you'll hear, "Have you ever thought about not struggling with that anymore?" Please. That's really unhelpful.

Sometimes we need to treat deep fear and anxiety like a broken arm and not be ashamed to get a cast for it. Get help. Get treated. Get counseled. We have amazing resources for anxiety and depression. Why should we be ashamed to use them? That's definitely running toward the roar with the help of trained professionals at your back. But I want to talk about what happens when fear and anxiety come into being where they previously were not. Where there was not any illness. Where peace used to be.

I'm talking about fighting fears instead of feeding them.

To an extent, you have cognitive horsepower in your mind that you have to choose to allocate to worry. But it can't be allocated to worry and to worship at the same time.

We've chosen as a culture to accept worrying as the new normal, as though we had nothing to do with it, but we shame those who suffer into silence. We don't speak about it, and so many people are looking to answers that can't possibly give relief. Opioids. Drug abuse. Alcohol. Addiction. Suicide.

Honestly, I'm furious about it. And I want you to be mad about it too. I want you to be filled with indignation at the thought of what the devil wants to steal from you and the way he bombards you with crippling fear and anxieties.

This war being waged within, we know full well the Enemy is behind it. And that's why it is essential you keep up the fight. Because you have an Enemy that's fighting against you. As much as God is for you, the devil is opposing you and wants to wipe you out, take you out.

There needs to be some fire in your spirit, because this life is not an amusement park. It's a battleground. The stakes are high, and there are people everywhere we need to reach. And you have to have a different mentality. Once you've declared war, your mentality shifts. Once you realize, *Oh, my gosh! These are not peacetime conditions,* you live smarter and you make smarter choices on a day-to-day basis.

CONTROL WHAT YOU CAN

In today's verse, Paul's talking about the camps of the enemy. Snipers are looking for elevated positions, right? The enemy wants the high ground so he can shoot down on you. So to keep that from happening, you have to hold the high ground. You have to keep control of your heart, your emotions, your mind. These are the theater of war.

We talked about things like worship and prayer and scripture reading that give you the high ground. The supernatural power of God gives us our strength, and we can't fight without connecting to him. But I think even little, boring, everyday things are important too. Like sleep. And hydration. And what you start and end your day with. That's why I want to give you one more small but pointy weapon to fight with through the night. I call it 8–8–8.

What does that mean?

What if you got eight hours of sleep on average a night? I know sometimes you're going to get four, but you could try and get nine the next one. What if your goal was eight uninterrupted hours of sleep?

What if your goal was eight glasses of water a day? It would be better than

ONCE YOU'VE DECLARED WAR, YOUR MENTALITY SHIFTS.

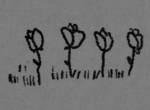

two sodas and a LaCroix and three cups of coffee. Eight would be better than whatever you're doing normally.

What if the first and last eight minutes of every day were given over to Jesus? Would you even recognize the version of yourself you would become? I mean, think about it. Think about how dysfunctional we become through lack of sleep. Think about dehydration, crankiness, and headaches. Think about how you're going straight to social media in the morning and ending with *The Walking Dead* at night. Still wondering why you can't sleep? Well, you watched someone eat someone else's face off two minutes ago. Of course you can't sleep! I'm not saying you need to watch *Little House on the Prairie* all day. I'm just saying, guard the first and the last. Just eight minutes. Set the bar low and grow from there. But start with something that's not intimidating.

If you start and end your day with Jesus, drink more water, get more sleep, and take care of the basics in your body, I'm telling you, your fears and nighttime anxieties would lessen. You can do that. And God will never do for you what you can do for yourself.

These are tiny tactical tweaks that can be the difference between living and dying on the battlefield.

Starve your fear.

Feed your faith.

Memorize some of the verses I lovingly placed at the back of this book. You will have them on difficult days. Be ready to pull them out when you need to shank the Enemy. Shank him with that toothbrush! Stick him with the pointy end! I take nothing from the devil anymore. I mean, I just go straight for the jugular, speaking the name of Jesus over the situation.

I'm not messing around. There's way too much I want to see God do in my day to give one more second over to fear and worry and narcissism and loneliness and all these things that cause wheels to spin and darkness to grow. Honoring God, speaking life to ourselves, and blessing people are things that bring joy. Let's hold the high ground however we can and keep fighting in ways large and small. Let's keep staring in the face of the things we're afraid of. Only then will we experience the rush that comes from prying joy from the clenched fist of fear. And looking back at the end of our lives, at every step we took forward into the face of our fear, we'll know it was worth it.

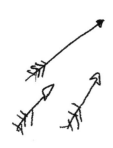

Prayer

Father, take every one of my thoughts under your control and in obedience to you. I can't control every circumstance of my life, but teach me to control what I can and surrender the rest to your nonstop care. Amen.

 ## BREATHE, THINK, AND LIVE

- x Revisit week 4, "Run Toward the Roar." How has your attitude toward your fears changed over this process?
- x Try 8–8–8 for a few days. How does it change things?

- In what ways has your fight been practical as well as spiritual? How do those two things go hand in hand?
- What fears or anxieties typically keep you up at night? Which shanks can you hide under your mattress to deal with those? Pick some from the scripture bank in the appendix and commit them to memory.
- In what ways have you found yourself running toward the roar recently? In what ways do you still want to make that your automatic response?
- What has your fight-or-flight instinct been telling you in the weeks of this journey? How will you dig in?
- How are you letting go of fear of failure? In what ways will you run toward the roar and go for the jugular?
- How have your strongholds been affected by this journey? In your experience, what have been the most lethal weapons in that fight?
- How have you experienced the effects of confession or bringing your junk to the dump? What has God been teaching you through it?
- How do other people and serving the church play a role in running toward your roar? What role would you like them to have going forward?
- In what ways has the Devil tipped his hand with your fears? How will you continue to pursue this?

Day 40

HHT THHT HHT HHT
HHT THHT HHT HHT

GET UP AND SHOW UP

Blessed is a man who perseveres under trial; for once
he has been approved, he will receive the crown of life
which the Lord has promised to those who love Him.

James 1:12 NASB

Larry Waters had a healthy fear of ice. He'd been around it and lived near it long enough to know it wasn't anything to play around with. And that's why he parked at the edge of the lake and unloaded his four-wheeler and decided to take that across instead of the heavier vehicle.

With his wife, Chrissie, sitting behind him, he cautiously began the journey across the lake, noticing that in the layer of snow that covered the surface there were tracks from cars that had evidently gone through it rather recently. And so he assumed if heavier cars and trucks could make it across, then he could on the much smaller, lighter vehicle.

He was making his way across, but at the halfway mark he heard and felt at the same time the ice cracking and the vehicle jolting. And then it pitched forward. Before he knew it, it had stopped, dropped, and rolled straight into the icy waters below the lake.

The vehicle sank to the bottom like a stone, but Larry and Chrissie managed to separate themselves. Still, they were floundering in that hole. Both of them instinctively made their way to the edge and sought to do what all of us would do at the edge of a pool: pull themselves out. But on the frozen edge, they just couldn't get a grip. No matter how they tried, their hands kept slipping off the ice.

Soon their hands were numb. They were clawing at the edge, and they couldn't do the one thing they were telling their hands to do: pull them out. With their wet clothes and filling shoes, they were heavier than normal. They began to realize, *We're going to die here today.*

Larry swam over to Chrissie, and with his few moments of life remaining, he gave her a kiss and told her he loved her, and they accepted that they were going to die cold and afraid, but together. We're going to leave them there for a while (don't worry; they survive—Larry is the one telling us about this story, after all), but we'll come back to them.

Larry's and Chrissie's words and emotions have rung true for me on so many days. Worries, fears, griefs, and insecurities have left me feeling completely and totally helpless in the dark, as if I were sinking into freezing cold water. Fighting and growing and victory in my calling seemed like distant dreams.

I've wanted to give up so many times. Maybe you've been there too.

But please, I'm begging you, don't give up. You've got to fight. You've got to keep fighting. And then, after that, here's what you do: keep showing up. That is the fight. Just keep showing up every day.

Here's another story, and you won't believe how it turns out. It's the story of the Leatherman Tool Group. They make a simple pocketknife that has pliers in it. You could take for granted a pocketknife with pliers. But it didn't exist until it did. Tim Leatherman was on a trip to Europe with his wife right after college, and their Fiat kept breaking down.

He had a Boy Scout knife and a pair of pliers that he kept fixing the car with. And he said to himself, *If only they had one that combined the pliers with the pocketknife. That would be amazing. Because then I wouldn't have to change hands.* He got home from the trip and decided to make it.

But it was easier said than done. Two years into the project, in his brother-in-law's garage, on his birthday, he broke down weeping because he couldn't get the pliers and the pocketknife to behave. But he said, "The next morning, I got up and I showed up. And I kept going."

Three years later a patent was issued for what we know of today as a Leatherman. We'd think, *Patent! Happily ever after!* But that's not how it went. For five years, no one bought it.

Every retailer, every hardware store, every company rejected it. They said there was no market for it. The Stanley company, the one that makes thermoses, told him no one would ever go for it. It was too much of a knife for the tool companies and too much of a tool for the knife companies. In all he received five hundred rejection letters.

Tim was distraught. After seven years he almost gave up. But a friend encouraged him to keep going. He said he'd work with him and maybe help him find something he hadn't thought of yet. So they kept going. Eight years later, Cabela's, a little-known company, said, "We'll buy five hundred." By this point, they had the sense to name the tool Leatherman. Cabela's put them on the market, and the rest, as they say, is history. The company is now headquartered in Portland and employs more than four hundred people. There are dozens and dozens of different models, and they sell $100 million worth of Leathermans annually.

It's a tale as old as time. A great company success story. Some of you might even have one. They're passed down from father to son, generation to generation. His success has spawned an industry; a whole new category of multitools from different companies now imitate his original idea and are ubiquitous in hardware and sporting goods stores.

Think about what it took for Tim Leatherman to keep showing up for all those years when everyone was telling him, "This'll never work." That war, that doubt, alone in that garage, on his birthday, weeping, wanting to give up, wanting to quit. Some of you can relate.

I wonder, where are you at on that journey? What are you thinking about quitting? What do you think about giving up? What dream are you beginning to lose faith in?

Here's the truth: this is a fight. It's not just one round and it's over. It's not just, "Well, there, I fought. I tried to control my thoughts. I tried to speak differently. I tried to plant the church. I tried to write the sermon. I tried to start the business. I tried to work on the marriage." That's not a fight!

A fight is bloody round after bloody round. A fight is getting knocked down and getting back up again. A fight is spitting your tooth out in the sink! A fight consists of going from failure to failure to failure to failure without losing your enthusiasm.

I want to speak life over your tomorrow. Throughout this journey, starting in week 1, I have been trying to convince you of your identity and your calling. To remind you that God loves you, has a plan for you, wants to do more through you than you can ever imagine. That he wants to reach others through your story in lifesaving ways. He's got your back as you grow toward that. All of it's true, and believing it changes everything. But even after you believe it, you've got to fight!

What about Larry and Chrissie? We left them drowning in the lake. They kissed goodbye. But just before Larry began to sink, he felt a Leatherman in his pocket. And God only knows why or how he thought of it, but he opened it and, using the pliers, he was able to dagger the edge of the ice and pull himself up and out. He immediately pivoted and was able to pull his wife to safety. I imagine they're grateful Tim Leatherman never gave up.

Yes, you are fighting a difficult, bloody battle. You are trying to win the war within. But you are not the only one. There are people all around you, people in your family, people in your life, people you don't even know yet, and they're trying to win it too. If you give up, how will God ever use you to reach them?

In the garage, through the years of slogging it out, Tim never knew about Larry and Chrissie. But God knew that his showing up and not giving up was going to lead to rescue for other people.

As you continue to fight the good fight and keep living, it's not just for yourself you must fight to take back your life. God wants to save lives through you. You're not the only one trying to win the war within. Who knows what your legacy will be if you keep getting up and showing up tomorrow and the next day and all the days after that.

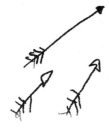

Prayer

Father, use me for your glory! Remind me that it's not about me; it's all about you. I choose today to buckle down and fight so that Jesus will be made

BREATHE, THINK, AND LIVE

- x What tends to numb you and stop you from this fight?
- x How are you going to keep up the dogged determination to keep going?
- x What are the Leathermans in your pocket that can get you out of whatever hole you're in?
- x How does the fact that you could be someone's Leatherman change the way you look at your setbacks and failures?
- x Look back at week 5, "Be the Difference." How do you see your pack growing and strengthening through this process?
- x How have you been letting people in? How do you hope to keep doing that in the future?
- x In what ways can you seek out encouragement from your pack to keep

going in this journey? How can you set up a multi-wolf pregame howl to keep you amped in this fight to take back your life?

x What are you most excited about when you think about the encouragement you could contribute and the role you could play in the lives of those around you?

x Think about using your words and self-management for the good of the pack. How have facing issues of anger, irritation, rudeness, and interpersonal messes changed the way you look at those around you?

x How is staring down and addressing those issues better than avoiding them? What new pathways might this open up in your relationships?

x How is your posture changing, internally and externally? How do you hope it will continue to change?

x If you've asked the Holy Spirit into your relationships, how are you finding the path? How will you continue to go to the source for your power?

AFTER

Seven Years in Heaven

This morning I didn't need an alarm to get me out of bed. The calendar in my head woke me up. Today is December 20. A day that represents sorrow and beauty. Joy and mourning. Profound loss and even more surprising gain.

Seven years ago, my daughter Lenya left this world and went home to heaven after a shocking and sudden health crisis that emerged from out of nowhere. This morning—and the other 2,554 times I have woken up since that day—the temptation has been to feel like my daughter is behind me. But the truth is that she is in front of me, and I am moving closer to being reunited with her all the time. Things are not as they seem. Objects in the mirror are closer than they appear.

Seven years feels like a significant period of time. Somehow it feels substantial in a way that three or four or even nine years doesn't. A whole week of years. Just as in Scripture the number forty stands for a period of testing, the number seven in the Bible speaks of something being full or complete. Genesis explains that in seven days God created the world. The book of Joshua tells us that the Israelites marched for seven laps around Jericho before its walls fell. Isaiah talks about seven ways the Holy Spirit works.

My favorite seven in the Bible is that John's gospel records seven different times Jesus said the words "I am." He used this loaded phrase, which hearkens back to God's self-disclosure to Moses on Sinai, to make it clear that he—Jesus—is the God who created the world in seven days. Each of those uses of the words *I am* was followed by clarifiers like "the bread of life" (6:35) or "the good shepherd" (10:11) or "the way, the truth, and the life" (14:6). Every day for seven years, I have been buoyed by the remembrance that he also declared himself to be "the resurrection and the life" (11:25). The flexibility of "I am" shows that within Jesus' identity is room for all of your deficiency. He is whatever you need, and he is whatever you're not.

You have now made it through the forty days of testing, and I commend you for it. You are well on your way to taking back your life—from narcissism, from anxiety, from dysfunction, from pettiness, and from living a small story centered only on your journey when there is an infinitely big God who has invited you to be a part of his never-ending plans and glory. There will be many, many times when you feel like you don't have what it takes, and in those moments when you want to throw up your hands and declare that you're not enough, remember that God is whispering to you, "I am."

What is my reward for coming to this milestone of seven years? The same as yours in coming to the end of this journey: we get to begin again, one day at a time. And we must never give up. Satan, who kills and steals and destroys, would love to take your life or trick you into taking your life, but through Jesus you have the power to take back your life from the things that would hold you back or knock you out. You must stay the course. The best is yet to come.

From now on, I want you to take a different view of the difficulty that you will inevitably face. American poet Robinson Jeffers wrote, "In pleasant peace and security / How suddenly the soul in a man begins to die." There is a gift inherent in trials that keeps you sharp as a razor's edge. Complacency can set in when you lose the fight in your soul. Kings become fools when they stop going out to battle. When you understand that, you stop praying for a lighter burden and start praying for a stronger back.

Teddy Roosevelt's love of war, which led to his wolf-rising moment that we talked about on day 15, began when he was very young. Teddy saw his father respond to the Civil War draft by paying a proxy to fight in his place—a common occurrence among people who had the money for it. Teddy's father (nicknamed Great Heart) paid for the proxy after being begged by his wife, Mittie, to not fight in war. She was from the South, and she couldn't bear to see him take up arms against her homeland. He regretted it all his life. In Teddy's estimation, it was the only thing his dad ever did that was not heroic.

I want to apply that concept to you on two levels. First, in the fight to take back your life, no substitute can fight these battles for you. No one can walk with God on your behalf. Either you drop to your knees and pray, love, and serve other people, or you don't. It's the small choices that no one but you will know about that will lead you to the life that everyone wants.

Second—and much more important—take comfort from knowing that the greatest battle has already been fought for you. Jesus stepped into your place and died on the cross on your behalf. Because he was separated from the Father, you never will be. Because he died, you now live. God made him who knew no sin so that we could become the righteousness of God in him. On your best day and on your worst, God sees in you the perfection of Jesus. Knowing that changes everything. You don't need good works to earn God's approval. You have God's approval, so now you are opened up to a life of good works.

When both of these truths are at play—God's ability and your availability—two oceans are connected. No longer are you trudging around continents, enslaved to moods and emotions and your circumstances. This "canal" bridges land with living water and opens you up to a brand-new way to be human. Here's to the grand adventure of grace, one day at a time!

ACKNOWLEDGMENTS

It takes a village to release a book. This interactive journey is no exception.

I'd like to thank Debbie Wickwire for the idea to take the core messages and deleted scenes from *I Declare War* and *Through the Eyes of a Lion* and put them in a format that could help the message get down deeper into the cracks of people's lives. I am so excited to finally be printed in hardcover—and with a ribbon!

Thank you, Jennifer McNeil, for combing through books and sermon notes and transcripts for gems buried and long forgotten. You did a magnificent job giving new life to forgotten truth.

Thank you to Meaghan Porter for editing my work and (as always) making it appear to the world like I speak English.

Thanks, Austin Wilson, for representing me well and for getting in the cold plunge!

And to my remarkable team at Fresh Life who had a hand in this project: Mckenzie, Katelyn, and Elisha for another amazing cover, and Alie for being willing to chime in even from maternity leave.

Thank you, Jennie, for loving me on the days when I haven't done such a great job of taking back my life.

Thank you, Liv, Daisy, Clover, and Lennox, for keeping me sane and making me eager to get home. Thank you, Lenya, for always reminding me where my true home and my treasure are. And thank you, Tabasco, for being the most loyal and spicy miniature poodle around.

And to you, the reader of this book, thank you! I salute you for the step you have taken to lay hold of all that Christ Jesus laid hold of you for!

NOTES

Before

xi a six-hundred-page book David McCullough wrote about it: Unless otherwise noted, information about the Panama Canal is taken from David McCullough, *The Path Between the Seas: The Creation of the Panama Canal, 1870–1914* (New York: Simon and Schuster, 1978).

xi "one of the supreme human achievements of all time": David McCullough, quoted in Sean Mattson, "Panama Remakes its Famous Canal for Giant Ships," Reuters, November 17, 2009, https://www.reuters.com/article/us-panama-canal /panama-remakes-its-famous-canal-for-giant-ships-idUSTRE5AH02S20091118.

xvi "Water Displacement, perfected on the 40th try": "Fascinating Facts You Never Learned in School," WD-40 (website), accessed February 10, 2020, https://www.wd40.com/history/.

Day 1: Hiding in Plain Sight

3 In 2011, the FBI ended the most extensive manhunt: Steve Kroft, "Whitey Bulger's Capture—The *60 Minutes* Report," CBS News, November 24, 2013, https://www.cbsnews.com/news/whitey-bulger-the-gaskos-60-minutes/.

Day 2: Identity Crisis

12 "You cannot outperform or underperform": Jason Selk, *10-Minute Toughness: The Mental Training Program for Winning Before the Game Begins* (McGraw-Hill Education, 2008), Kindle.

Day 4: Tortured Genius

23 "A person who is exceptionally intelligent": Lexico.com, s.v. "genius," https://www .lexico.com/en/definition/genius.

23 **"No one is a genius all the time":** Seth Godin, *Linchpin: Are You Indispensible?* (New York: Penguin, 2010), introduction, iBooks.

Day 5: If You Say So

33 **"The doors of hell are locked on the inside":** C. S. Lewis, *The Problem of Pain* (1940; repr., New York: HarperCollins, 1996), 130.

Day 6: Mask Off

37 **"We cannot selectively numb emotions":** Brené Brown, *The Gifts of Imperfection: Let Go of Who You Think You're Supposed to Be and Embrace Who You Are* (Center City, MN: Hazelden, 2010), 70.

Day 10: Lenya Lenses

64 **"walking around with your heart outside your chest":** Meg Meeker, MD, *Strong Fathers, Strong Daughters: 10 Secrets Every Father Should Know* (Washington, DC: Regnery, 2006), 60.

67 **the things of this world grew strangely dim:** Lyrics paraphrased from Helen H. Lemmel, "Turn Your Eyes upon Jesus," 1922.

Day 11: Bread and Circuses

73 **"For the People who once upon a time handed out military command":** Juvenal, Satire, 10.81.

Day 12: The Harm of Being a Hybrid

76 **the lions "are extremely weak":** Palash Kumar, "Lions Dying in Indian Zoo After Failed Experiment," Reuters, September 6, 2006, http://bigcatrescue.org/lions-dying -in-indian-zoo-after-failed-experiment/.

Day 13: Pain Is a Microphone

83 **"God whispers to us":** C. S. Lewis, *The Problem of Pain* (1940; repr., San Francisco: HarperSanFrancisco, 2001), 91.

Day 15: Over the Line

98 the "power of joy in battle": Theodore Roosevelt, "A Colonial Survival," *The Cosmopolitan* 14 (November 1892–April 1893), 232.

99 he "became the most magnificent soldier I have ever seen": Edmund Morris, *The Rise of Theodore Roosevelt* (1979; repr., New York: Random House, 2001), 674.

100 "The moment one definitely commits oneself": William Hutchison Murray, *The Scottish Himalayan Expedition* (London: J. M. Dent, 1951), 7.

Day 17: Flip Your Thoughts

114 "Before battle of fist must come battle of mind": *Kung Fu Panda 3*, directed by Alessandro Carloni and Jennifer Yuh Nelson (20th Century Fox Home Entertainment, 2016), DVD.

115 In the book *Extreme Ownership: How US Navy SEALs Lead and Win*: Jocko Willink and Leif Babin, *Extreme Ownership: How US Navy SEALs Lead and Win* (New York: St. Martin's Press, 2015), 199.

Day 18: Mind Your Words

119 "Well, the Jerk Store called": *Seinfeld*, season 8, episode 13, "The Comeback," directed by David Owen Trainor, written by Gregg Kavet and Andy Robin, featuring Jerry Seinfeld and Jason Alexander, aired January 30, 1997, on NBC.

122 sixteen thousand words come out of your mouth per day: Richard Knox, "Study: Men Talk Just as Much as Women," NPR, July 5, 2007, https://www.npr.org/templates/story/story.php?storyId=11762186.

Day 19: Change the Outcome

128 He wrote *The Cat in the Hat* with 236 different words: Austin Kleon, *Steal Like an Artist: 10 Things Nobody Told You About Being Creative* (New York: Workman, 2012), 138.

130 A researcher from Harvard University discovered: "Study Reveals Referees' Home Bias," BBC News, May 6, 2007, http://news.bbc.co.uk/2/hi/uk_news/england/6629397.stm.

Day 20: Take Back the Controls

132 **"We are what we repeatedly do":** Will Durant, *The Story of Philosophy: The Lives and Opinions of the World's Greatest Philosophers from Plato to John Dewey* (1926; repr., New York: Pocket, 1953), 76.

133 **According to research from Duke University:** David T. Neal, Wendy Wood, and Jeffrey M. Quinn, "Habits—A Repeat Performance," *Current Directions in Psychological Science* 15, no. 4 (2006): 198.

134 **Americans spend up to five hours a day on our phones:** Sarah Perez, "US Consumers Now Spend 5 Hours per Day on Mobile Devices," TechCrunch, March 3, 2017, https://techcrunch.com/2017/03/03/u-s-consumers-now-spend-5-hours -per-day-on-mobile-devices/.

134 **"bright dings of pseudo-pleasure":** Paul Lewis, "'Our Minds Can Be Hijacked': The Tech Insiders Who Fear a Smartphone Dystopia," *Guardian*, October 6, 2017, https://www.theguardian.com/technology/2017/oct/05/smartphone-addiction -silicon-valley-dystopia.

135 **"He read seven languages":** David McCullough, *The American Spirit: Who We Are and What We Stand For* (New York: Simon and Schuster, 2017), 27.

136 **"Sometime, somewhere along the line":** McCullough, *American Spirit*, 42.

136 **Those who commit their goals to paper:** Mary Morrissey, "The Power of Writing Down Your Goals and Dreams," Huffington Post, updated December 6, 2017, https://www.huffingtonpost.com/marymorrissey/the-power-of-writing -down_b_12002348.html.

Day 21: Compound Interest

138 **Physicist Hans van Leeuwen discovered:** Sean Treacy, "Dominoes: More Powerful Than You Think," *Inside Science*, January 30, 2013, https://www .insidescience.org/news/dominoes-more-powerful-you-think.

139 **"Good and evil both increase at compound interest":** C. S. Lewis, *Mere Christianity* (1952; repr. New York: HarperOne, 2001), 133.

142 **"Whenever anyone makes an important change":** Bernard Roth, *The Achievement Habit: Stop Wishing, Start Doing, and Take Command of Your Life* (New York: HarperCollins, 2015), 105.

143 **"If you can break a habit into its components":** Charles Duhigg, *The Power of Habit: Why We Do What We Do in Life and Business* (New York: Random House, 2012), 20, 62.

Day 22: The Nearest Lion

150 **"Aye, fight and you may die":** "Are You Ready for War," *Braveheart*, directed by Mel Gibson (1995; Hollywood: Paramount Home Video, 2002), DVD.

Day 23: Let It Go

154 **It took Bruno Mars an entire year:** Bruno Mars, interview with Lara Logan, "Bruno Mars on His Artistry: 'I'm Working Hard for This,'" *60 Minutes,* CBS News, June 11, 2017, https://www.cbsnews.com/news/bruno-mars-on-his-artistry-im -working-hard-for-this/.

155 **"Just keep swimming":** *Finding Nemo*, directed by Andrew Stanton and Lee Unkrich, Disney/Pixar, 2003.

157 **"Laces out, Marino!":** "Wow! Ray Finkle's House," *Ace Ventura: Pet Detective*, directed by Tom Shadyac (1994; Burbank, CA: Warner Home Video, 1999), DVD.

Day 24: Terror by Night

165 **experiencing three or more incidents of intense stress within a year:** Daniel Goldman et al., *Harvard Business Review: On Emotional Intelligence* (Harvard Business Press, 2015).

165 **"The strength of the Pack is the Wolf":** Rudyard Kipling, *The Second Jungle Book* (Leipzig: Tauchnitz, 1897), 33.

Day 26: Use What You've Got

175 **There's a great scene in *Iron Man 3*:** *Iron Man 3,* directed by Shane Black, Marvel Studios, 2013.

178 **In *Black Hawk Down*:** *Black Hawk Down,* directed by Ridley Scott, Revolution Studios, 2001.

178 **"Satan trembles":** William Cowper, "What Various Hindrances We Meet," *Olney Hymns* (London: W. Oliver, 1779), no. 60.

Day 28: Hope Has a Rope

188 **"Physicians can often tell the moment":** Meg Meeker, MD, *Strong Fathers, Strong Daughters: 10 Secrets Every Father Should Know* (Washington, DC: Regnery, 2006), 189.

191 **"Grab a root and growl":** R. Douglas Hurt, *Documents of the Dust Bowl* (Santa Barbara, CA: ABC-CLIO, 2019), xxiii.

Day 29: Stay in the Pack

195 **"They care for their pups":** Jim and Jamie Dutcher, *The Wisdom of Wolves: Lessons from the Sawtooth Pack* (Washington, DC: National Geographic, 2018), 20–21.

Day 30: The Power of the Howl

202 **the book *The Wisdom of Wolves*:** Unless otherwise noted, information about wolves in this chapter is taken from Jim and Jamie Dutcher, *The Wisdom of Wolves: Lessons from the Sawtooth Pack* (Washington, DC: National Geographic, 2018).

202 **experts estimate:** Julian Fields, "Nonverbal Communication: How Body Language and Nonverbal Cues Are Key," Lifesize (website), February 18, 2020, https://www.lifesize.com/en/video-conferencing-blog/speaking-without-words.

204 **"an exuberant display of affection":** Nate Blakeslee, *American Wolf* (New York: Crown, 2017), 99.

Day 31: Don't Kick the Beehive

209 **"If you want to gather honey":** Dale Carnegie, *How to Win Friends and Influence People* (1936; repr., New York: Pocket, 1998), 3.

209 **"Participants who were treated rudely":** Christine Porath and Christine Pearson, "The Price of Incivility: Lack of Respect Hurts Morale—and the Bottom Line," in *Everyday Emotional Intelligence: Big Ideas and Practical Advice on How to Be Human at Work* (Cambridge: Harvard Business Review, 2018), eBook.

209 **"people who'd observed poor behavior":** Porath and Pearson, "The Price of Incivility."

Day 32: Four Squares for a Better You

215 **"If we are going to be true to ourselves":** Lysa TerKeurst, *It's Not Supposed to Be This Way: Finding Unexpected Strength When Disappointments Leave You Shattered* (Nashville: Nelson, 2018), 165.

217 **"Almost all research now indicates":** Gary Chapman, *Anger: Taming a Powerful Emotion* (1999; repr., Chicago: Moody, 2015), 86.

218 **"If you speak when angry":** Authorship of this saying cannot be definitively determined, but a likely author is Groucho Marx, who is reported to have given this advice to a contestant on a TV show. See "Speak When You're Angry and You'll Make the Best Speech You'll Ever Regret," Quote Investigator, May 17, 2014, https://quoteinvestigator.com/2014/05/17/angry-speech/.

Day 33: Rise High, Bow Low

225 **When I was researching wolves:** Wolf facts in this chapter are taken from Jim and Jamie Dutcher, *The Wisdom of Wolves: Lessons from the Sawtooth Pack* (Washington, DC: National Geographic, 2018).

225 **Amy Cuddy's TED talk:** Amy Cuddy, "Your Body Language May Shape Who You Are," TEDGlobal 2012, Edinburgh, Scotland, June 2012, https://www.ted.com/talks/amy_cuddy_your_body_language_shapes_who_you_are?language=en.

226 **people respond in kind:** Sebastian Gendry, "Urban Myth: It Takes More Muscles to Frown Than to Smile," Laughter Online University, accessed April 24, 2018, http://www.laughteronlineuniversity.com/true-false-takes-43-muscles-frown-17-smile/.

Day 35: Pencils Down

238 **the origin of the word *deadline*:** Online Etymology Dictionary, s.v. "deadline," https://www.etymonline.com/word/deadline.

241 **"What we do in life echoes in eternity":** "Far From Home (Main Title)," *Gladiator*, directed by Ridley Scott (2000; Universal City, CA: DreamWorks Home Entertainment, 2000), DVD.

Day 40: Get Up and Show Up

275 **the story of the Leatherman Tool Group:** *Made of Mettle: The Leatherman Documentary*, YouTube video, uploaded by Leatherman, July 16, 2018, https://www.youtube.com/watch?v=rvCgGgokH_E.

After

280 **American poet Robinson Jeffers wrote:** Robinson Jeffers, "The Cruel Falcon," 1935.

281 **Teddy Roosevelt's love of war:** Edmund Morris, *The Rise of Theodore Roosevelt* (1979; repr., New York: Random House Publishing Group, 2010), Kindle.

APPENDIX: SCRIPTURE TO MEMORIZE

Here are some incredible passages to focus on when you need to evict troublesome thoughts. Each will fill your mind with peace and force out the thoughts you are trying to remove in the same way that pouring water into a pitcher forces out all the air.

Let love be without hypocrisy. Abhor what is evil. Cling to what is good. Be kindly affectionate to one another with brotherly love, in honor giving preference to one another; not lagging in diligence, fervent in spirit, serving the Lord; rejoicing in hope, patient in tribulation, continuing steadfastly in prayer. (Romans 12:9–12)

Love never gives up.
Love cares more for others than for self.
Love doesn't want what it doesn't have.
Love doesn't strut,
Doesn't have a swelled head,
Doesn't force itself on others,

Isn't always "me first,"

Doesn't fly off the handle,

Doesn't keep score of the sins of others,

Doesn't revel when others grovel,

Takes pleasure in the flowering of truth,

Puts up with anything,

Trusts God always,

Always looks for the best,

Never looks back,

But keeps going to the end. (1 Corinthians 13:4–7 THE MESSAGE)

But the fruit the Holy Spirit produces is love, joy and peace. It is being patient, kind and good. It is being faithful and gentle and having control of oneself. There is no law against things of that kind. Those who belong to Christ Jesus have nailed their sinful desires to his cross. They don't want these things anymore. (Galatians 5:22–24 NIRV)

For where envy and self-seeking exist, confusion and every evil thing are there. But the wisdom that is from above is first pure, then peaceable, gentle, willing to yield, full of mercy and good fruits, without partiality and without hypocrisy. Now the fruit of righteousness is sown in peace by those who make peace. (James 3:16–18)

O God, You are my God;
Early will I seek You;
My soul thirsts for You;
My flesh longs for You
In a dry and thirsty land
Where there is no water.
So I have looked for You in the sanctuary,
To see Your power and Your glory.

Because Your lovingkindness is better than life,
My lips shall praise You.
Thus I will bless You while I live;
I will lift up my hands in Your name.
My soul shall be satisfied as with marrow and fatness,
And my mouth shall praise You with joyful lips.

When I remember You on my bed,
I meditate on You in the night watches.
Because You have been my help,
Therefore in the shadow of Your wings I will rejoice.

My soul follows close behind You;
Your right hand upholds me. (Psalm 63:1–8)

But also for this very reason, giving all diligence, add to your faith virtue, to virtue knowledge, to knowledge self-control, to self-control perseverance, to perseverance godliness, to godliness brotherly kindness, and to brotherly kindness love. For if these things are yours and abound, you will be neither barren nor unfruitful in the knowledge of our Lord Jesus Christ. (2 Peter 1:5–8)

Finally, be strong in the Lord and in his mighty power. Put on the full armor of God, so that you can take your stand against the devil's schemes. For our struggle is not against flesh and blood, but against the rulers, against the authorities, against the powers of this dark world and against the spiritual forces of evil in the heavenly realms. Therefore put on the full armor of God, so that when the day of evil comes, you may be able to stand your ground, and after you have done everything, to stand. Stand firm then, with the belt of truth buckled around your waist, with the breastplate of righteousness in place, and with your feet fitted with the readiness that comes from the gospel of peace. In addition to all this, take up the shield of faith, with which you can extinguish all the flaming arrows of the evil one. Take the helmet of salvation and the sword of the Spirit, which is the word of God.

And pray in the Spirit on all occasions with all kinds of prayers and requests. With this in mind, be alert and always keep on praying for all the Lord's people. (Ephesians 6:10–18 NIV)

For your obedience has become known to all. Therefore I am glad on your behalf; but I want you to be wise in what is good, and simple concerning evil. And the God of peace will crush Satan under your feet shortly.

The grace of our Lord Jesus Christ be with you. Amen. (Romans 16:19–20)

Since Jesus died and broke loose from the grave, God will most certainly bring back to life those who died in Jesus.

And then this: We can tell you with complete confidence—we have the Master's word on it—that when the Master comes again to get us, those of us who are still alive will not get a jump on the dead and leave them behind. In actual fact, they'll be ahead of us. The Master himself will give the command. Archangel thunder! God's trumpet blast! He'll come down from heaven and the dead in Christ will rise—they'll go first.

Then the rest of us who are still alive at the time will be caught up with them into the clouds to meet the Master. Oh, we'll be walking on air! And then there will be one huge family reunion with the Master. So reassure one another with these words. (1 Thessalonians 4:14–18 THE MESSAGE)

The Lord is my shepherd;
I shall not want.
He makes me to lie down in green pastures;
He leads me beside the still waters.
He restores my soul;
He leads me in the paths of righteousness
For His name's sake.

Yea, though I walk through the valley of the shadow of death,
I will fear no evil;
For You are with me;
Your rod and Your staff, they comfort me.

You prepare a table before me in the presence of my enemies;
You anoint my head with oil;
My cup runs over.
Surely goodness and mercy shall follow me
All the days of my life;

And I will dwell in the house of the Lord
Forever. (Psalm 23:1–6)

Let not your heart be troubled; you believe in God, believe also in Me. In My Father's house are many mansions; if it were not so, I would have told you. I go to prepare a place for you. And if I go and prepare a place for you, I will come again and receive you to Myself; that where I am, there you may be also. And where I go you know, and the way you know. (John 14:1–4)

ABOUT THE AUTHOR

LEVI LUSKO is the founder and lead pastor of Fresh Life Church, located in Montana, Wyoming, Oregon, and Utah. He is the bestselling author of *Through the Eyes of a Lion*, *Swipe Right*, and *I Declare War*. Levi also travels the world speaking about Jesus. He and his wife, Jennie, have one son, Lennox, and four daughters: Alivia, Daisy, Clover, and Lenya, who is in heaven.

New Video Study for Your Church or Small Group

If you've enjoyed this book, now you can go deeper with the companion video Bible study!

In this five-session study, Levi Lusko helps you apply the principles in *Take Back Your Life* to your life. The study guide includes video notes, group discussion questions, and personal study and reflection materials for in between sessions.

Study Guide
9780310118916

DVD with
Free Streaming Access
9780310118930

Available now at your favorite bookstore,
or streaming video on StudyGateway.com.